Homeless Families

Homeless Families

The Struggle for Dignity

Barry Jay Seltser and Donald E. Miller

University of Illinois Press
Urbana and Chicago

Library of Congress Cataloging-in-Publication Data

Seltser, Barry Jay.
    Homeless families : the struggle for dignity / Barry Jay Seltser and Donald
E. Miller.
        p.   cm.
    Includes bibliographical references and index.
    ISBN 0-252-02021-9 (cloth : alk. paper).—ISBN 0-252-06327-9
(pbk. : alk. paper)
    1. Homeless persons—California—Los Angeles.   2. Homelessness.
I. Miller, Donald E. (Donald Earl), 1946–   .   II. Title.
HV4506.L67S45 1993
305.5′69—dc20   92-46062
                                                                              CIP

Home is where one starts from.
— *T. S. Eliot*

To our parents,
Charlotte Gale Seltser and
Raymond Seltser
and
R. Elizabeth Miller and
Glenn E. Miller

Contents

Preface

This book is about homeless people, but it is addressed to those who are fortunate enough not to be homeless. It is a book about events that author and reader alike will probably never experience, about struggles most of us will never live through. Although we will be pleased if homeless people read these pages, the book is written not to them, but about them and for them.

This difference between the reader and the book's homeless subjects creates both possibility and peril. The distance allows us (both author and reader) to stand back from the subjects' painful and frightening experiences, to gain some perspective on the recent increase in the number of homeless families, to think through the implications of our response to homelessness, and then to empathetically identify with the lives of homeless people. Indeed, we write this book precisely to take a small step toward breaking down the barriers to understanding and compassion.

However, the distance also creates the danger that we will remain aloof, considering these experiences to be so alien to our experience as to be either unintelligible or unworthy of serious concern. After all, for those likely to read this book, life is too steady, predictable, and balanced to allow easy identification with the lives of homeless families. Just as we are tempted to cross to the other side of the street when confronting a destitute person who might make some demand on us, so we may avert our attention from the social and economic factors that create homelessness.

The greatest challenge in writing this book has been to find a way to reaffirm both the distance and the identification, the uniqueness and the universality of the experiences we seek to describe. Most of us have never been homeless, are unlikely to become homeless, and cannot easily put ourselves in the shoes of homeless people and know what their lives are like.

But, at the same time, there are elements in the experiences of homeless persons with which we *can* identify. The task is to translate these experiences into our language, to find the common denominators of our lives that allow us to recognize that what is happening to them is a quintessentially human experience. Those of us reading this book may not be homeless, but we are nevertheless susceptible to life-threatening diseases and experiences that challenge our self-sufficiency and reveal our personal vulnerability.

This book combines empirical and moral analysis in order for us both to understand some of the experiences of homeless families and also to ask ourselves what these experiences can and should mean to us as citizens of the United States in the 1990s. In collecting the data for this book, we have attempted to observe the canons of impartial social science research. But we also believe that interpretation of data inevitably is done from a vision of what is desirable and humanly possible. Indeed, the greatest figures in sociology have all possessed a moral vision of what constitutes a good society.

Therefore, rather than grudgingly admit that description is always tinged with prescription, we self-consciously examine homelessness from a moral perspective. Specifically, we are interested in the ways in which homelessness attacks the dignity of its victims and the ways in which mediating institutions, such as shelters or the social service system, either restore dignity to homeless families or else contribute to the attack on their dignity. Thus our approach in this book moves back and forth between description and prescription, in part because of our conviction that social problems such as homelessness require both careful description and impassioned critical response. In this regard, perhaps a few words about the academic backgrounds of the two authors will clarify for the reader our dual commitments to social science research and moral analysis.

Both of the authors are trained in the field of religious social ethics, an academic discipline heavily influenced not only by Christian theology and Western philosophy but also by twentieth-century social scientific theory and research into the contexts in which ethical decisions are made. Both of us chose this path of study because of long-standing interests in moral reasoning and empirical research, and these interests have continued to influence the way in which we think and write.

Barry Seltser has a doctoral degree in both sociology and religious ethics and has spent the past thirteen years examining the ways in which ethical decisions are lived out within organizational and cultural settings. He wrote a dissertation on the topic of commitment to work, examining how and why managers in modern America dealt with the demands of their employing organizations and the ways in which these demands either complemented or threatened their other commitments to family, leisure, or personal identity. He also wrote a book on the process of political compromise in the U.S. Senate, seeking to understand why politicians were so willing to compromise with each other and whether there were any principles or ideals located beyond the political process that were uncompromisable. In his teaching, he focused on applying the resources of both theological and social scientific traditions to understanding the ways in which people and groups could act ethically in the midst of pressures and demands created by their social contexts.

Donald Miller earned his undergraduate degree in psychology, and his doctoral work was in social ethics. He recently finished a book on the Armenian genocide of 1915, which is based on in-depth interviews with one hundred elderly survivors of the massacres and deportations that took place in Ottoman Turkey. He is currently involved in two research projects: one is a two-year study of rapidly growing neofundamentalist churches; the other project is an examination of responses of the religious community to the recent Los Angeles riots. Both projects reflect many of the same methodological commitments as the present study on homeless families, including a strong emphasis on in-depth interviewing and extensive observations of religious settings. In his courses in the sociology of religion he focuses on the importance of moral and theological issues in the interpretation of social and religious change.

Several years ago both of us became fascinated and troubled by the growing problem of homelessness, particularly by the apparent increase in the number of homeless families. Our interest was in part an academic one: we viewed this problem as an important opportunity to ask some difficult questions about values and moral action in modern American urban society.

But we acknowledge a more basic—and more troubling—motivation for addressing this problem: namely, our own personal responses to confronting individual homeless people in our daily lives. Both of us were uncomfortable with our feelings of discomfort and embarrassment and by our all-too-common reactions of denial and avoidance. Do you give money when approached on the street or when called on the phone by an advocacy group? Do you talk to someone who is sleeping on a street grate?

We suspect that these tensions apply to most of our readers as well. The ways in which most of us are confronted with the problem of homeless people are not conducive to easy solutions or moralistic arguments on either side. And that is precisely why it is important to take the time to look directly at the experiences of homeless people in terms of what they can tell us about our own values. Our response in morally ambiguous situations is the best gauge of our underlying ethical commitments; nothing is likely to challenge a comfortable self-assured ethical identity as much as a sudden and uncomfortable confrontation with someone who is homeless and hungry as we are leaving a restaurant or are on our way to a secure job or the comforts of a home.

At a less personal level, examining the experiences of homeless people reveals a great deal about our political culture. We believe the old truism that a society can ultimately be judged by the way it treats those at the bottom of its social structure, and homeless families represent that population in stark ways. Precisely because most of these people are single women with children, they are likely to be perceived as the most vulnerable among us, with little power and few resources to take control of their lives. How we (both as individuals and as a society) respond to them speaks directly to the actual moral commitments we are prepared to embody in our lives. The choices are not easy, of course, and the policy decisions are seldom clean. But the mere existence of families struggling in extreme poverty challenges many assumptions about our country and our way of life.

We hope that this book, written in full awareness of the complexity and frustration these issues raise for all of us, will both inform and motivate readers to respond to the poorest members of our society. The voices of the homeless women and men in these pages can help us understand ourselves and our moral commitments as well as what it means to experience poverty and homelessness. As the authors, we make no claim to be responding more "correctly" than anyone else. Indeed, it is precisely our awareness of falling so short that has sparked our commitment to this project. We merely hope that we can share with the reader some of what we have learned about the experiences of being homeless—and some of the moral implications of that awareness.

As we penned the final words to this book, the Los Angeles riots took place. Having observed firsthand the results of the looting and the burning of stores, it is impossible not to inquire into the link between what we learned about homelessness in Los Angeles and the riots. The decade of the 1980s saw a dramatic widening of the gap between rich and poor in Los Angeles. While looting is not morally justified, the frustration of people who are caught in a downward economic spiral can be appreciated. The riots are rightly interpreted as class-based, rather than race-based, warfare. In this regard, the homeless families of Los Angeles are simply an extreme symptom of a much larger urban crisis.

Nevertheless, while social class is an important variable in understanding the riots, so is the issue of human dignity—the focal point of this book. If blacks in Los Angeles had a history of being treated with dignity by the police as well as their fellow nonblack citizens, it is difficult to imagine that the Rodney King verdict would have ignited the social disorder that occurred. But the sad reality is that in spite of the civil rights legislation of the 1960s, blacks of all classes are frequently treated without respect. Hence our focus in this book on homeless people's struggle for dignity has a much wider application.

While social commentators have written much about Los Angeles as a trend-setting city, especially as the movie and entertainment capital of the world, the city may also be a trendsetter in terms of social problems. Conditions of violence in south central Los Angeles rival those of any city in the United States, and the multiplicity of different ethnic groups and cultures in Los Angeles is one of the greatest anywhere. For that reason, Los Angeles is an excellent laboratory in which to examine the possibility of human beings relating to each other with dignity and respect.

Acknowledgments

In completing this book, we recognize the extent to which the names on the title page fail to reflect the engagement and energy of so many others whose thought and time are responsible for the finished product. Most important has been the willingness of the homeless people in our study to speak with us. Whatever success we have had in probing and explaining the experience of homelessness is a result of their honesty, concern, and openness.

In addition, we are particularly grateful to Alice Callaghan, the director of Las Familias del Pueblo, who had the original vision for this book and who secured the funding for the interviewing, transcription of tapes, and initial analysis of the data. She has been a continuing source of emotional support for this project, although we do not wish to hold her responsible for any of the views expressed in these pages.

The workers and managers of the five shelters we visited were also inspirational sources of wisdom and guidance, and they eased the always-difficult process of arranging and conducting interviews. The promise of anonymity to the subjects of this study precludes us from mentioning shelter personnel or organizations by name.

Emily Culpepper, a former social worker and currently a professor at the University of Redlands, conducted most of the interviews, and the quality of the data is largely due to her combination of intellectual rigor and emotional insight. Wendy Parham, a graduate student in social ethics at the University of Southern California, also did a limited number of interviews in Spanish, and we are grateful for her assistance.

Numerous other people in the Los Angeles area—social workers, public officials, and advocates—gave generously of their time and advice as we struggled to understand the lives of homeless families. In particular, we would like to recognize Kay Young McChesney, whose dissertation at the University of Southern California on homeless women and children provided important guidance in the construction of our interview guide.[1]

We are particularly grateful to Kai Erikson for providing extremely valuable reactions to this book (he waded through the manuscript twice, a sign of his well-known generosity). In addition we are grateful to Kevin Ennis, David Tripp, and Bill Sabol for reading the manuscript and offering valuable suggestions. We also thank Richard Martin, our acquiring editor at the University of Illinois Press.

Homeless Families

Introduction

The purpose of this book is to help the reader understand the experience of homeless families in the United States—and respond to it. We have tried to listen to and interpret what homeless families told us about their lives, their problems, and the wider society in which we all live. By interviewing one hundred families living in homeless shelters in Los Angeles, we hoped to provide a window into the experience of being a homeless parent and to glimpse (however briefly and imperfectly) what it means to be homeless.

Homelessness is a strange and complex problem for most of us. In approaching this social world, we must bear in mind two important and closely related distinctions. First, all human experiences have both an objective and a subjective dimension. Our lives have characteristics that can be described from the outside, and that can be perceived and responded to by others. At the same time, we experience our lives from the inside, with all the attendant pleasure, pain, uncertainty, and confusion that entails. When we are speaking of a set of experiences most of us have never undergone, we must be especially aware of the distinction between objective and subjective approaches. In order to understand what homeless people are experiencing, we must seek to fathom not just the facts and patterns and events of their lives but the ways in which they feel and respond to these events as human beings.

Second, any social situation can be viewed from both a descriptive and a moral framework. Description requires a certain amount of distance, of dispassion, in seeking to ascertain the facts and get them right. When we are dealing with complex social and political problems, though, we can (and usually do) approach our social world from a moral perspective as well. We ask not simply what happens, but whether it should happen; not only why someone feels a certain way, but what our responsibility may be for those feelings; not simply how someone became homeless, but whether it should have been avoided.

As we examined hundreds of pages of interview transcripts, the theme of dignity began to emerge as a central component of the experiences of our study's participants. The common thread in their stories is the affront to their sense of personal dignity and self-respect. This theme is particularly important for homeless parents, who often interpret their inability to provide stable shelter for their children as a deep personal inadequacy. Although usually submerged, the question that appears to gnaw at the spirit of these mothers and fathers is, Why is it that other parents are able to provide for their children, but I have failed? Many things can be taken from persons without breaking their spirit, but the loss of a sense of dignity is particularly tragic.

Because this book is about dignity, it is impossible to make the distinctions between objective and subjective, between descriptive and moral, in any neat way. Objectively, we can attribute dignity to people, either because they are human beings or because they are seen to act in certain ways. Subjectively, we experience our own lives as possessing or lacking dignity, depending upon how others treat us and how we understand ourselves. But our inner feelings are influenced by how others respond to us, and those responses often depend on objective assessments they are making of our lives.

Similarly, on a descriptive level, we can point to specific facts—how someone acts, how we feel toward that person, how that person feels—as revealing and reaffirming a person's dignity. We can identify specific acts and feelings that reveal a dignified or undignified way of responding or of living. But we are led immediately to the deeper moral questions of whether certain people deserve to be treated in particular ways, of how we should be acting toward them, of what their rights and our obligations may be. Indeed, when we refer to someone as having dignity, or a right to dignity, we are moving to this more explicitly moral dimension.

Dignity, therefore, is a "bridge" concept, forcing us to move back and forth between objective and subjective viewpoints, between descriptive and moral analysis. When we describe the external experiences of homeless families, we are not merely pointing to external events—we are also exploring the ways they think and feel about themselves and the underlying moral significance of their lives. In listening to them, and in discussing their experiences, we have to introduce moral concerns into our primarily descriptive discussions; we must report not only what happens to people but how they feel about it. To do otherwise is to radically separate what cannot be separated. We are interested in how homeless families experience their own dignity—and in how the rest of us uphold or threaten that dignity by the ways in which we respond to them, both as individuals and as a society.

This book moves broadly from a more objective to a more subjective perspective and from a primarily descriptive to a primarily moral perspective. Many of the subjective and moral themes developed in detail in the later chapters are foreshadowed as we listen to people recount what has happened to them. We hope our readers will keep an open mind and an open ear for the various levels of analysis.

Part 1 introduces the reader to the broad picture of homeless families and their experiences. Chapter 1 presents an overview of some of the facts concerning homelessness in the United States and a description of the people who were interviewed. Chapter 2 examines the stories of five of our respondents, seeking to provide both a description of their life stories and a better understanding of the complex and intertwined causes of homelessness.

Part 2 remains primarily at the descriptive level, and it focuses on two objective contexts within which these homeless families live that affect both their external situations and their inner feelings. Chapter 3 looks at the welfare system, asking how this institution sustains or undermines the dignity of homeless families. Chapter 4 turns to the shelters in which our respondents were living at the time of their interviews. Similarly, it illustrates the ways in which shelters support or threaten the dignity of their residents.

Part 3 moves to a more subjective level, examining some of the ways in which homeless parents cope with and make sense of their experiences. Chapter 5 identifies various defense mechanisms of distancing through which they struggle to maintain their sense of dignity. Chapter 6 deals with the role of religious explanations in enabling them to interpret and give meaning to their experiences.

Part 4 focuses on the moral perspective. Chapter 7 includes a conceptual discussion of dignity and how it relates to the experiences of homeless people, and it offers some suggestions about various broader cultural values that affect the ways in which we respond to homeless families. In Chapter 8 we draw together many of the book's earlier themes and ask what they can tell us about the social and individual obligations we have toward homeless families.

In short, we hope to contribute to a discussion of the moral basis for relating to homeless persons and to illuminate the complex ways in which our experiences shape, and are shaped by, our underlying value commitments, both as individuals and as a society.

PART ONE

The Experience of Homelessness

1

Families: The New Face
of Homelessness

Beginning in the 1980s, the old image of the homeless person—a male alcoholic living on Skid Row—changed. A new group of homeless became more visible, one made up of children and their parents. Although accurate statistics are difficult to determine, perhaps one-third of the homeless in America are families, and as many as one hundred thousand children are homeless every night.[1] The "New Homeless," as they have been called, differ in important ways from traditional images of the homeless as tramps or vagrants.[2] The profile of a typical homeless family in the 1990s reveals a single mother in her late twenties or early thirties, living on welfare or minimum-wage income, with one or two small children. She is a member of a minority group, and this is her first experience of being homeless.

Generalizing about the demographic characteristics of the homeless population should be done with some caution, however, because all races and family types are represented. In a recent study in northern California, a team of Stanford University researchers found that 36 percent of 809 homeless families were Hispanics of Mexican descent, 25 percent were blacks, and 29 percent were non-Hispanic whites. They also discovered that although slightly more than half of the families were headed by single parents, both biological parents were present in 30 percent of the families.[3] Thus homeless families are a diverse group, with whites and traditional two-parent families being substantially represented. Perhaps the best generalization one can make is Kathleen Hirsch's powerful comment that "there are no typical homeless people, only common suffering."[4]

In understanding homelessness in America, it is also important to guard against stereotypes that are uncritically accepted. For example, it is simply not true that once a family is homeless, it will remain that way for years. Summarizing research on this issue, a 1991 Children's Defense Fund report states that "most families are homeless for less than thirty days."[5] Likewise, a common misperception is that most homeless families are recent newcomers to the community, either from out of state or from another country. In fact, numerous studies have found that homeless families are a relatively geographically stable population; for example, the Stanford researchers discovered that the homeless people they interviewed in San Francisco had lived there for an average of twelve years and that those living in San Mateo and Santa Clara had lived there for an average of nine years.[6]

Some of the stereotypes associated with homeless individuals are unfortunately generalized to homeless families, and this confluence of perceptions is also often erroneous. Indeed, the Stanford research team found important differences. Homeless parents were younger and less likely to have histories of drug abuse, alcoholism, or mental illness when compared to homeless individuals. The Stanford study also found that families tended to be homeless for a much shorter period of time than individuals—one month versus one year. Also, for two-thirds of the families, this was the first time they had been homeless, compared to 44 percent of the individuals. Also noteworthy is the fact that Hispanic families were much less likely to have been previously homeless than the other populations in their sample.[7]

Becoming Homeless

In any particular case, it is often possible to identify a basic precipitating factor that resulted in a family becoming homeless. A relationship with a spouse or boyfriend went sour, eliminating an important source of income. A family was evicted from its apartment because the children were too noisy or disruptive. One of the family members—perhaps the father or an older sibling—used drugs, and the landlord evicted the entire family. And sometimes a parent was simply not a very good money manager, and a few weeks of overspending on food, toys, or clothing left a family without money to pay the rent at the end of the month.

Families who become homeless have few resources for buffering their descent onto the streets. They may stay with relatives for a few nights or attempt to borrow money from friends, but these are temporary solutions to a more fundamental problem. With no place else to go, a mother bundles her children into their last refuge, a dilapidated car, and here they spend a few uncomfortable nights. Alternatively, they may make their way to an inexpensive motel where they can pay by the day or week. But because such accommodations seldom have cooking facilities, the family is forced to eat in fast-food restaurants, and very quickly they are penniless. It is at this point that the reality of their situation becomes uncomfortably clear, and if this mother and her children are fortunate, someone refers them to a shelter, which hopefully has room to accommodate them.

Recent research undermines monocausal explanations for the rather dramatic increase in the number of homeless families today. For example, blaming homelessness on the increase in single mothers is simplistic. Women frequently end their relationships with husbands or partners out of desperation because of abuse. Very commonly drugs or alcohol are also involved. Because the family is already living on the margin of poverty, the resulting disruption in income after the break-up tips them over the brink into homelessness. Women who become homeless often do not have credit cards or established credit histories that would allow them to borrow money to ease the transition into a new life. Also, these single parents have often been reared in dysfunctional families and hence have no close family members to whom they can turn. Even if a relative or friend takes them in, it is often for only a few nights.[8]

In two-parent families, a variety of precipitating factors may account for homelessness. Many families rely on a parent's minimum-wage job and are always on the verge of not being able to pay their monthly rent. Loss of a job, a major medical problem, or illness can tip a family over the edge into homelessness. Also, the homeless population includes families that have moved to an urban center in search of a better life. With a few hundred dollars in their pockets and an aging car that is not too reliable, the parents head the family to Los Angeles or some other metropolis. Upon arriving, they discover that jobs are not as plentiful as they thought, and, equally important, housing costs are high. The relative who was going to help them in this new city soon extricates himself from any responsibility for their welfare. Within a matter of a few weeks, the family is living in a car, and in desperation it turns to a church or social service agency for assistance. The effort to begin a new life has turned to tragedy. To be homeless is a shocking reality that defies the family members' self-image as middle-class citizens.

Structural versus Individualistic Theories

The previous examples describe precipitating factors that explain how families become homeless, but it is equally important that individual cases be understood within the context of deeper structural explanations of homelessness. One must ask, for example, why families have been the fastest-growing population among the homeless in both the 1980s and the 1990s. Is homelessness to be attributed simply to irresponsible behavior? Or are there deeply rooted factors that make some people more likely candidates for homelessness than others?

Surely the answer to these questions is that individualistic interpretations of homelessness are incomplete unless they are nested in structural explanations.

In many cities homelessness is predictable without reference to individual life histories: there is simply a shortfall in the number of housing units, given the number of people seeking shelter; consequently, those with the least resources end up on the streets. In Los Angeles, where our research was conducted, the estimated shortfall is ten thousand housing units per year when one compares increases in population with available housing.[9] Rents have skyrocketed because of high demand and extremely low vacancy rates. In fact, they increased 110 percent from 1980 to 1988, far outstripping increases in the minimum wage or welfare payments.[10] Those on relatively fixed incomes are simply not able to compete in a rising tide of housing costs.

Nationally, the pattern related to homeownership and rental rates is rather startling. The 1991 Children's Defense Fund report cited earlier summarizes some of these trends.

—Nationally, rental costs (including utilities) rose 13 percent faster than inflation between 1973 and 1987, and rents rose 26 percent faster in the western states.
—In 1970 there were 8.5 million units renting at less than $250 a month (in 1987 dollars); by 1987 the number of units available at that price fell to 6.6 million.
—The median price of a house rose by more than 20 percent between 1973 and 1987 (in real, inflation-adjusted dollars), while median family income rose by less than 1 percent.
—Between 1974 and 1987 homeownership fell by 8 percent among all families with children, but the following categories of families were hardest hit, with homeownership falling
  —14 percent among female-headed families,
  —12 percent among black families,
  —17 percent among Latino families,
  —18 percent among young families (parents between the ages of 25 and 29), and
  —33 percent among poor families.
—In 1973 it took 23 percent of the median income of families (headed by parents less than thirty years old) to carry a mortgage on the average-priced house; in 1986 that mortgage required 51 percent.[11]

Hence, while it is easy to identify a precipitating factor to explain why one particular family became homeless, if there is a shortfall in housing units it is inevitable that some element of the population is either going to be homeless or else live in substandard housing. In Los Angeles, for example, it is estimated that 40,000 families are living in garages or other "shadow" housing and that 150,000 households spend over half their income on rent.[12] Indeed, among recent Hispanic immigrants, "hotbedding" is reportedly a common phenomenon, where several shifts of people take turns sleeping in the same bed.

Beyond this, a variety of economic factors conspire to create homelessness. The recession has increased joblessness, but an even more threatening phenomenon is the decline in the number of low-skill jobs. Many entry-level positions have been exported to third-world countries. Hence adults with marginal educational backgrounds find it difficult to achieve steady employment. Even a full-time minimum-wage job does not support a family of four above the poverty line.[13] The erosion of the middle class in America is seen nowhere more clearly than in the number of families who, because of a single precipitating event, become homeless.

The median income of the poorest fifth of the population dropped 11 percent between 1973 and 1987. And the income of young families took a precipitous drop. For those families (with children) headed by a person less than thirty years old, the average income dropped 24 percent. Young black families were hit even harder, experiencing a decline of 33 percent.[14] In California there was a 41 percent increase between 1980 and 1990 in the number of children under eighteen years old living below the poverty line. In 1990 1.3 million children in California were living in families with incomes that put them below the poverty line.[15] Nationally, in 1989 more than 12 million children, or one in every five, were living in poverty.[16]

Other factors behind the rise in homelessness include substantial cultural and economic changes affecting family structure. Many more children are being born into single-parent families now, and many more families are having to cope with divorce. Homelessness is becoming an increasingly common experience for women who formerly lived relatively stable middle-class lives. In 1989 children in female-headed households were five times more likely to be living below the poverty line than children living in homes with two parents.[17] Furthermore, the intergenerational support structure linking young adults, parents, and grandparents is more precarious than at any other time in the nation's history. In light of these developments threatening family stability, homelessness is just one expression of deeper changes occurring in American culture.

Research on homeless families is also making us increasingly aware of the amount of abuse, both sexual and physical, that fills the lives of the homeless.[18] Not only is domestic violence a precipitating factor for women terminating relationships, but it appears that many homeless mothers were abused as children. As adults these women may have difficulty creating long-term relationships with men and may choose to live with abusive men. Family homelessness is on the rise as women flee the violence inflicted by these partners.

Although structural explanations of homelessness check our dehumanizing inclination to blame individuals for becoming homeless, to reduce this problem simply to economic and cultural explanations is also dehumanizing because by doing so we fail to recognize the personal responsibility of individuals to choose and act. Stated differently, while social structural approaches avoid blaming the victim, they have the corresponding vice of denying the moral agency of the homeless person. Any approach to homelessness must hold these two perspectives in tension. Individualistic approaches to homelessness are inadequate unless they acknowledge structural factors that produce homelessness; at the same time, structural approaches to homelessness must recognize that most adults live in situations that, however constrained, continue to provide them with some personal choice and responsibility for their actions.

Interviewing Homeless Families in Los Angeles

Between October 1988 and March 1990 we and our assistants interviewed one hundred heads of households who were living with their children in several different shelters in Los Angeles. Staff at the shelters scheduled interviews for us with individuals who agreed to participate in this study on a voluntary basis.[19]

Because most of the participants were mothers,[20] we believed it was important for a female to conduct the interviews. Except for ten interviews conducted by Barry Seltser, all the interviews were handled by two women with backgrounds in social work. The interviews typically lasted forty-five minutes to an hour, and they were conducted in relatively private settings. Questions were asked from a structured interview guide (see appendix 3) and were open-ended in nature, allowing the participants to talk about their lives and feelings in highly personal terms. We believe that most participants in the study found the experience to be cathartic and even enjoyable, as the interview provided an occasion to talk about their problems and also their hopes and dreams for the future.[21]

We can make no claim that our sample is typical of all homeless families in Los Angeles, although the participants did represent a wide range of experiences and fit the general profile of more quantitatively oriented studies. Because most of the participants were residents in shelters with high admission standards, our sample may include families that were somewhat more functional than the homeless population as a whole. Consequently, in describing the characteristics of the interviewed families, we will focus on actual numbers of people rather than percentages, in order to remind the reader that our sample may not characterize the whole population of homeless families.[22]

The interviews were conducted in five diverse shelters, ranging from a large multistory facility to a small converted house servicing five or six families. These five shelters are among the best in Los Angeles, and to some extent we may assume that their residents represent the best-adapted members of the homeless population. Because they prohibit drug or alcohol use on their premises, and because of the strict shelter rules, people with severe emotional and physical addiction problems were excluded. Also, it is important to note that all the participants in our study were homeless persons with at least one child living with them in the shelter; excluded from our study were interviews with men or women who might have been parents, but whose children were not with them.

Characteristics of Study Participants

Nearly half of the participants were black and about one-quarter were white, with Hispanics, Native Americans, and one Filipino accounting for the remainder of the interviewees. All studies of homeless persons have found minorities to be disproportionately represented, and our study is no exception.[23] (Hispanics may be underrepresented in our study because we were able to conduct only a few interviews in Spanish.)[24]

Of those we interviewed, only twenty-eight persons were living with a spouse in the shelter. Eight additional individuals were not married but had partners with them in the shelter. Forty-two of the study participants were single unattached people. Another fourteen had a partner or spouse living somewhere other than in the shelter, and eight participants were married but completely uninvolved with their spouse. Our sample reflects the national pattern, which shows that many homeless families are headed by single parents.[25]

Forty of the parents we interviewed were 20 to 29 years old. Another thirty-eight were in their thirties. Fifteen of our respondents were over 40, including two who were over 50 years old. Six were under 20 years old. National studies of homeless families have shown the parents' age to be relatively young, and our sample is no exception.

A majority of the participants (65 persons) had only one or two children living with them in the shelter, a fact consistent with other studies of homeless families. In addition, seventeen women were pregnant at the time of the interview. While having children (especially young children) may make it difficult for mothers to work full-time, there is little indication in the literature that larger family size predisposes families to homelessness.[26] However, it is worth noting that thirteen participants had at least one dependent child currently living with another family member, a fact that reminds us of the ways in which family stability is threatened by homelessness.

Only one-third of the participants had not completed high school. The remaining individuals had high school degrees, and twenty-eight had done at least some college work, including eight with an associate's degree and two with college diplomas. While educational background may be a factor contributing to homelessness for some persons, it is striking that so many participants were high school graduates.

The class backgrounds of our sample were diverse, but they tended to be fairly high considering the fact that they were homeless when we interviewed them. Two-thirds of the participants said that their families had been financially secure while they were growing up. Only eleven people said that their childhood had been characterized by economically marginal circumstances, and only one person indicated that she had been homeless as a child. In fact, thirty-six of our study participants said that their parents had owned their own homes.[27] Also notable is the fact that fourteen individuals in our sample said that they had been homeowners at some point prior to becoming homeless.

By coding responses to open-ended interview questions, we were able to determine the precipitating cause of homelessness for most people in our sample, although in 13 cases it was difficult to identify only one issue. In 37 cases the participants indicated that they had simply run out of money and were unable to continue paying rent, at which point they were evicted by the landlord. In another 30 cases, the precipitating factor seemed to be the dissolution of a relationship with a roommate, boyfriend, or relative with whom they had been living, which forced them out of a stable living situation. Seven other individuals indicated that they were evicted from an apartment either because their children made too much noise or because there were too many children living in the apartment. Five people said that they were evicted when their welfare check did not arrive on time, and another five said that they were evicted because of drug use.[28] In three cases the precipitating factor was a serious illness or injury that precluded them from working.

We also coded descriptions of where the participants had been living immediately prior to entering the shelter in which they were interviewed. One-third of our sample had been living in another shelter. Over half (fifty-five persons) said that they had been living in a hotel or motel, paying either by the day or week, when their money ran out. Nearly a quarter (twenty-two persons) said that they had spent at least one night with their family on a park bench, beach, or street or in a parked car at some point before entering the shelter.

Finally, we attempted to identify recurrent personal and family problems that characterized the lives of the participants. Although we believe they were the best adapted of the homeless population, thirty-one people in our sample had been involved in relationships with partners who had serious drug problems. In fact, a quarter of those we interviewed admitted that they had used illegal drugs, although most maintained that this was not the reason they had become homeless. Similarly, about a quarter of our interviewees said that they had been involved in relationships with people who were alcoholics, although only six said that they, personally, had an alcohol problem.

One of the most notable findings was that forty of the mothers said they had experienced serious physical abuse as adults. They had been beaten, attacked, or threatened with knives or guns. In addition, twenty-one of our interviewees said that they had been physically or sexually abused as children.

Conclusion

In the next chapter, we will put faces to some of the statistics that we have just cited regarding our sample of respondents. The best way to understand the experience of being homeless is to chronicle the lives of individuals who find themselves in this circumstance. The causes of homelessness are complex, and generalizations about the population of homeless families are inadequate unless they are connected to the diverse lives of particular individuals.

2

Becoming Homeless
in Los Angeles

The typical television documentary on homeless families features a white, middle-class woman whose world fell apart when her husband walked out on her and their two small children. She is portrayed as a victim of circumstances that were beyond her control. The shelter, however, is helping her and the kids get back on their feet. She is enrolled in a community college program that will give her marketable skills. The kids are doing well and enjoy playing with the other children in the shelter. As the program proceeds, we place ourselves increasingly in her situation, wondering where to volunteer and how big the check should be to our local homeless shelter.

A few homeless mothers do fit this romanticized picture, but the actual ranks of the homeless present a much more complex image. Based on our one hundred interviews, the world of the homeless is filled with alcohol, drugs, violence, and sexual abuse. The children tugging at their mother's skirt are often from two different fathers, neither of whom may be present. Parents' poor planning and lapses of judgment may have led many families into living on the streets of Los Angeles. Unlike the typical television portrait, the homeless are often less like us than we are led to believe. Most of us have not had their difficulties, and, in listening to their stories, we are likely to think that we would not have made many of their choices.

What are the implications of shattering the media image of the "worthy homeless"? Does it mean that we should condemn and blame them for their behavior? Does it imply that welfare payments should be reduced, and lack of family planning made a capital offense? Does it mean that we should keep our hands in our pockets as we pass homeless people on the street who ask us for bus fare or money for a cup of coffee?

It is premature to answer these questions until we have put faces on some of the homeless people who were interviewed. We need to listen to them talk about their lives and tell of some of the experiences that give depth to their current situation. It is appropriate to encounter some of those persons the television cameras may have passed over. If we are going to ask about our moral response to the homeless, then we should move beyond superficial impressions.

We would reiterate our earlier insistence on maintaining both distance from and identification with these people's lives. Many of the stories told in this book simply underscore the ways in which our lives are insulated (in differing degrees, of course) from their situation. But their experiences are still human ones, and in numerous ways we are all vulnerable to similar threats and fears, if only in terms of a worst-case scenario for our futures. Anyone who has ever felt the wrenching threat of losing a job, or who has fallen behind on credit card payments, or whose children were directly exposed to violence or abuse can well empathize with the despair and emptiness that can define the daily lives of homeless people.

In listening to and responding to the stories told by these homeless people, two points may be helpful. First, these stories are just accounts of events, not history. We are not particularly concerned with whether the events happened precisely as described. It is impossible to determine accuracy to that extent, and our concern in this book is primarily with the subjective experiences these people have in trying to make sense out of what happens to them. They are trying to give us an interpretation, a picture, of what has occurred, and why. Accounts may tell us more about the needs and interpretive styles of the respondent than they do about the exact events that occurred.

Second, it is helpful to view these people as survivors who are undergoing difficult experiences. Their words are intended not only to inform us of facts but to make us appreciate how painful and difficult these experiences have been. Like survivors everywhere, they need to share with us their personal understanding of their lives, as well as the ways in which they have adapted and carried on in the midst of the pain. Such a perspective allows them to educate us about how human beings deal with difficult trials, and it can enable us to enter into their world.

When we first began our analysis of the interviews, we attempted to develop a typology of different patterns of homelessness. But after struggling with the stories, we recognized that these peoples' lives were too complex to lend themselves to such a method, which would obscure more than it would reveal about their experiences. Therefore, we present several accounts as indicative of the sorts of stories we heard. The five portraits that follow may not be typical of all homeless families in America, but they do reflect the broad range of accounts that we heard in our interviews. We have occasion-ally altered specific details (such as the state where someone was born or where someone worked) only when that was necessary to protect confidentiality; otherwise, the stories are presented as we heard them.

Betty Reynold

Homeless people are poor, and many of them have been poor all their lives. But most poor people are not homeless, and we need to ask about some of the events that move people into homelessness. Betty Reynold's story brings us face-to-face with someone who might not have become homeless except for a series of events that she experienced as being out of her immediate control.

Betty Reynold is a thirty-nine-year-old divorced black mother with four children, living in a shelter with her two youngest boys (who are eleven and six years old). Ms. Reynold has always been poor. She grew up in the deep South, where her parents rented a place for fifteen dollars a month: "Back there, the white folks had everything and the black folks had nothing, you had to take what you could get. So we had to chop cotton by the wagon for three dollars a day." Her mother died when she was eight, forcing her and her sister to leave school to work so that her brothers could continue their education. Uneducated and unable to write, she left her family's home when she turned eleven and had her first child when she was fourteen. She moved to Los Angeles five years later, and she moved back home for a while before returning to California about ten years ago.

She has lived in various low-income apartments over the years, usually relying on her AFDC (Aid for Families with Dependent Children) check and food stamps. Without a steady job for the past twenty years, she has struggled to find and keep affordable apartments. She had recently managed to find a nice apartment in another part of California, where she was living with her two younger sons and her twenty-year-old daughter. She was poor, as she had always been, but she was settled.

The slide into homelessness began a year ago, when her daughter began using drugs. One day Ms. Reynold refused to give money for drugs to her daughter, whose response was to start breaking the windows in the apartment. Around the same time, her daughter's husband became extremely jealous of the daughter's boyfriends, and started coming around and shooting a gun on the street. Finally, she took the few hundred dollars she had managed to save and came to Los Angeles with her two sons, planning on moving in with her sister until she found an apartment.

But the sister's husband had just been released from jail, and there was not enough room for them to stay longer than a month. She moved in briefly with her brother and then into a house with a friend of her brother's. But he turned out to be a loud and threatening alcoholic, so she was forced to move into a motel for a week, and her AFDC money quickly ran out. She was unable to receive any special homeless assistance money from the state because she had given some of her AFDC money to her son, who had just gotten out of prison: "I don't care, the money there is for me too. I can do what I want [with it], and I'd rather help my son. [The welfare people] got mad and told me I wasn't eligible for [homeless assistance money], and I still haven't gotten it."

She took her children to the Skid Row area to look for a cheaper apartment or hotel, but the area was too dangerous. She was afraid to expose her children to all the drugs and violence: "My kids couldn't stay in no place like that. No ways. My kids were seeing things, I was seeing things that I never known was true, you see on T.V., you never know things like that happen." Having nowhere else to turn, she ended up in another shelter for one month before moving into the one where she was interviewed.

What was responsible for her homelessness? Listening to the story, we can pick from a series of equally plausible factors: severe and long-term poverty, lack of education and job skills or experience, drug use by her daughter, her family's inability (or unwillingness) to provide her with a place to live, and her insistence on giving money to her son. Other factors may have been equally important, such as having so many children at such a young age, the lack of a stable relationship with a partner, and the fact that the AFDC payments in her southern state were too low to allow her to move back there, where the housing is much less expensive.

There is no single cause for her homelessness. For many reasons, Ms. Reynold has lived almost all her life just one step away from being on the streets. Indeed, it is irrelevant which of the many more immediate factors—her daughter's drug use, her son's prison release, the high cost of housing in Los Angeles—was the single most important one in finally making her homeless.

More important than any specific cause is the overall trajectory of her life. We are listening to someone who might not be homeless at all but for a run of bad luck and too few resources (either personal or financial) to protect herself. In retrospect, we are tempted to view her earlier relatively secure life as unusual, wondering why she didn't end up homeless even earlier.

Rosa Hernandez

Mrs. Rosa Hernandez's life has been one disastrous episode after another. She is a twenty-five-year-old Hispanic woman, born in Los Angeles in a small family with both parents present. Her father always worked, usually driving trucks, and her parents rented decent apartments. But she remembers that they both used drugs and alcohol: "Everything was different. . . . Sometimes everything would be normal, and then sometimes everything would be—kind of like *this*." Her father was extremely violent, beating and sexually abusing her and her siblings, threatening to kill them, and repeatedly severely beating their mother. The children were finally taken away from home when Rosa was twelve.

Even when her siblings were allowed to return to their mother, she was forced to go to a girls' home. "I was different," she explained. She was treated as a runaway and a juvenile delinquent. Eventually able to move back with her mother, she quit school in the ninth grade and began working in a fast-food restaurant, a job she lost when she allowed one of her brothers to steal some food. She worked in various minimum-wage jobs after that and became pregnant at age eighteen. Moving in with her new daughter's father, she found she had jumped from one bad situation into another: "Oh God, he was worse than anybody I ever met. . . . He was violent, he was a mama's boy, he was a baby, he was sick, he was a wimp. . . . I don't see how I spent that much time with him, I guess it was about two and a half years." She finally left him and married her current husband soon thereafter. They have a young child of their own, a daughter, and Mrs. Hernandez is now pregnant again.

Recently the Hernandezes had been staying with one of Rosa's cousins, but they were thrown out after repeated arguments between her two children and the cousin's young children. Given no warning, they moved in with one of her sisters, who was about to give up her apartment, thus forcing them to move out very quickly. Her mother offered to let them stay with her in her trailer home, but it was much too crowded, so she ended up sleeping in the car with her husband and her two children for several nights before coming to the shelter.

Mr. Hernandez has both alcohol and drug problems, including intravenous drug use, which has been going on since he and Rosa met each other. She thinks he has stopped drinking heavily, although he still occasionally gets drunk on beer and has become violent to her and other people when drunk. He has been in and out of jail on drug-related offenses, and his drug use continues. Mrs. Hernandez cannot ask anyone for help for fear that they will be evicted even from this temporary shelter. She says: "He won't even acknowledge that there is a problem. He tries to ignore the fact that he's even doing it. I ask him about it, he tells me lies and says that he's not. I can see marks on his body, I know he's doing it, I know, I can tell, I know it as well as if I did it with him."

Although she worked briefly before having her first daughter, Mrs. Hernandez has relied primarily on AFDC ever since, and she has not held a job for almost six years. Mr. Hernandez has worked sporadically driving a truck, making a bit more than minimum wage, but he has had problems keeping a job, and his wife suspects that he is selling drugs. He has no regular job now and often spends two or three days away from the family with no explanation. Although worried about it, Mrs. Hernandez appears to prefer not knowing what he is doing; she insists that she has tried to control him but has failed to alter his behavior.

Mrs. Hernandez would like to find an apartment but complains that it is hard to afford anything large enough. She seems not to know about some of the housing assistance provided by the state, and she has had a difficult time receiving even basic benefits, such as food stamps, from her social worker. Her ambivalence about her current husband is reflected in the way she speaks about looking for another apartment in the Los Angeles area: "In a way I don't want to move over there because it's too easy for my husband to get to drugs. Anyways, I think for myself, I'm just going to not bother with him. I mean, I'm damned because I can't stop him, so I think I'm going to move back to L.A., get a house, make my own plans." She recognizes that her greatest need is to become "more aggressive in life, because I think this has caused me a lot of problems, just sitting back and relaxing." She does not want to stay on AFDC and hopes to become more independent: "One of my biggest mistakes in becoming homeless is to depend on my husband, in not being . . . more aggressive."

If we ask for an explanation of this family's homelessness, a host of equally plausible responses immediately leap to mind. Mrs. Hernandez has a history of abusive relationships with men and is currently involved with a man who, in addition to having serious addictive problems, has beaten her and is unable or unwilling to provide financial support by other than illegal means. She is untrained for work, trying to provide for two young children, pregnant, and dependent upon welfare and food stamps for her survival. She is living in a shelter, but she is afraid that she and her children will be thrown out if her husband is caught selling drugs.

Such stories immerse us in the very dense world of the extremely poor and the underclass of American society, where social and personal problems appear virtually insoluble. After all, where do we begin, as individuals or as a society, to help someone locked into such a long-standing and interwoven set of unhealthy and restrictive life choices and patterns? Mrs. Hernandez appears to be a classic victim of so many different social problems—physical and sexual child abuse, child neglect, abusive adult relationships, drug and alcohol abuse, poor job training and low wages for unskilled workers, a welfare system that provides little more than grudging financial assistance, expensive housing—that it is hard to imagine her breaking out of the cycle in which she has lived for so long.

Rachel Myer

In contrast to the stories of Betty Reynold and Rosa Hernandez, Rachel Myer's story appears to be a simpler one. It is easier to distance ourselves from stories of lives lived on the edge, composed of intertwined disasters and failures, particularly for those of us who can tell a much more stable and focused story about our own lives. It is the more "normal" stories of people such as Rachel Myer that may force us one step closer to recognizing the connection between these lives and our own.

A forty-one-year-old white woman living in a shelter with her black husband and their twelve-year-old son, Mrs. Myer's housing problems began when she became seriously ill while living in another part of the country. She had been employed as a nurse, and her husband, Tom, was a skilled laborer who made a very good salary. They rented a house for quite a while, and then an apartment, for which they paid seven hundred dollars a month rent for almost two years.

But she became ill with cancer and chose to come to the Los Angeles area to receive special medical treatment. Instead of separating the family for several months, which would have enabled Mr. Myer to keep his job and the apartment, they decided to remain together, quit their jobs, sell what they owned, and move here.

In Los Angeles, her cancer went into remission, but everything else in their lives began to fall apart. Mr. Myer was unable to find a job that would pay him what he had been making before; he believed he suffered from racial discrimination in looking for work, and he was hesitant about accepting a minimum-wage salary. Mrs. Myer was unable to get regular work because of the schedule of her treatments and the fact that she didn't have a car. The family stayed with a relative briefly, but the living conditions were too confining, and they moved into a hotel.

At that point, Mr. Myer broke his hand when he intentionally put his fist through a wall in frustration over his job prospects, and Mrs. Myer had to work seven days a week traveling all over the county on buses in order to find nursing work. As she says, "I was going all over, and I was working a lot, . . . so it was really a desperate situation, that I wasn't getting enough [work] but I couldn't afford to take the time off of the little bit of work I did get to go and try to find something else. . . . I know I cannot go a year working seven days a week, and so it was a real desperate situation."

Unable to stay at the motel without Mr. Myer's income, the Myers asked for help and were admitted to the shelter. But within a few days, Mrs. Myer slipped getting on the bus to go to work and seriously sprained her ankle. Thus neither of them could work, and their disability checks did not arrive quickly enough to help them save enough money to look for another apartment. They then had repeated problems with the welfare system and were unable to receive either AFDC or medical benefits either because of system delays or because of problems with their mailing address.

Both of the Myers are estranged from most of their relatives and have not asked them for assistance during this period. Indeed, Mrs. Myer has not even told most of her immediate family (many of whom are financially quite well off) about her illness, for fear that they will either become overprotective or won't care enough to do anything. Both of the Myers come from fairly poor backgrounds, and Mrs. Myer reports some serious problems with mental illness earlier in her life. Mrs. Myer comes from a very large family, and her father was physically incapacitated for most of her rather unhappy childhood; Mr. Myer's parents were divorced when he was quite young, and he also had a financially uncertain upbringing.

But their situation was very different from that of Ms. Reynold and Mrs. Hernandez. Mr. and Mrs. Myer both received some college education and were able to live fairly economically stable lives until her illness. When they were both working, they had a combined income of approximately $20 per hour, which amounted to well over $30,000 a year. She indicates how new this entire experience of homelessness has been: "We were coming from more or less almost a middle-class background, and so this whole situation is not in our element, and it's been really hard, some of the things we had to deal with and the people we've come in contact with." Had she not become ill, they would probably be living in their apartment, working at their respective jobs and raising their child. She describes their life before her illness as "pretty stable," and there were no drug, alcohol, or abuse problems to interfere with their fairly normal life.

In contrast, the past financial and emotional instability of their lives—coupled with their alienation from their families, possible job discrimination against Mr. Myer, and the uncertainty of their disability and welfare benefits—combined to make it harder for them to rebound from the series of physical problems that beset them. It is also worth noting how these illnesses and injuries began to mutually reinforce one another: the initial illness created a context of frustration, which led to Mr. Myers's broken hand, which then forced her to scramble constantly on buses to work long hours in diverse parts of the city, contributing to her falling and putting herself out of work. It is very common to find people in a situation where one misfortune is just enough to undercut the security and stability that existed previously, and the result can then be a deluge of events that are both effects of what happened before and causes of what is to come. It is clearly the interaction of the various forces that seem to conspire to both create their homelessness and make it more difficult for them to climb back out.

Sally Johnson

We look next at another person whose story seems to involve a similar combination of social and personal problems. Ms. Johnson is a thirty-three-year-old black woman living with her two daughters, one of them less than a year old. She came to Los Angeles several months earlier from another large city, where she had been living with her mother after her divorce because housing expenses were so high. Knowing several people in the Los Angeles area, and with some money saved up, she moved here and ended up in a cheap hotel where roaches were crawling on her daughter's face and where the manager offered to lower her rent if she would have sex with him. Afraid that her daughter would be harassed by either the manager or other people on the street, she kept her inside the room most of the time, leading her daughter to feel trapped: " 'I'm like a prisoner in here, why are you keeping me in jail?' Because the place was bad. I was scared for her to go outside. I kept the T.V. on to go to sleep."

She was unable to move anywhere else, however, because she had no income aside from AFDC and food stamps, and this was not enough for her to find a better place to live. Refusing to rely on her friends for help, she says: "I figured it's something I had to deal with on my own. I can't just go to a person and say, 'I'm having this problem.' " She assumed the friends would not have had room for her and her children, so she ended up in a shelter, then for a month in a tent city for the homeless in Los Angeles, and finally back in the shelter.

Ms. Johnson grew up in a relatively stable family setting. Her father was a sanitation worker and her mother was employed in a government office, and she and her seven siblings were well provided for in a home owned by her parents for twenty years. She lived at home until she graduated from school with an associate degree in business, and she held various electronics repair jobs, making almost $12,000 a year in her last job. Although this was not a large salary, she reports that she was able to live fairly well, but she decided to move back in with her mother in order to save money.

She had a drinking problem when she was a teenager, but otherwise she has not experienced any difficulties with drugs, alcohol, abuse, or mental illness. Until she moved to California, in fact, her story was a relatively straightforward account of someone becoming educated, working hard, and depending on her family to help her avoid the expense of high rent payments.

If we ask ourselves why she became homeless, two diametrically opposed types of responses are equally plausible. The high cost of housing in her earlier residence influenced her decision to move, and the problems with finding a stable and safe apartment or hotel in Los Angeles forced her into the streets. On the other hand, we might be led to ask why she chose to move to a part of the country with extremely unaffordable housing, particularly when she had lined up neither a job nor a place to live before coming out here with her two young children.

Is it a case of blaming the victim to ask these questions about her decision?

Perhaps, if the implication is that she is therefore at fault for her present situation. Ms. Johnson says she was treated that way by the welfare office, which tried to deny her AFDC benefits when she first moved: " 'Why did you ever leave? Well, you should have stayed there.' It was degrading enough that I had to go down there [to the welfare office]. . . . [They had an attitude] like I just came out here to collect welfare, which is ridiculous."

But it seems equally inappropriate to assume that her decisions, and the way in which she made them, were not factors in her homelessness. Unlike so many of our other shelter residents, she had a relatively stable upbringing, some advanced education and specific job skills, a solid work history, and a family (both in the earlier city and in Los Angeles) seemingly able and willing to help her out. It would be odd to deny that she is homeless now at least in part because of poor planning and her unwillingness to rely on people who might have supported her.

We can recognize the role she played in becoming homeless without blaming her for the result. After all, it may be perfectly understandable why someone would choose not to rely on her relatives to help her through a difficult situation, just as we can probably identify with the tendency to make a spontaneous decision to move without covering all the bases beforehand. We do not need to judge her actions, but we can point to the ways in which (according to her *own* account) her decision-making style and priorities have been a significant factor in landing her and her daughters in a shelter.

Mary Carter

We may feel uncomfortable drawing attention to the individual factors that seemed to affect Ms. Johnson. Are there some people for whom the broader social issues of affordable housing are clearly the source of their problems? Let's look briefly at the family in our sample for whom this would appear to be most clearly the case.

Mary and Tom Carter and their four children (three through twelve years old) moved to Los Angeles from Alabama several months earlier, hoping to have relatives find Mr. Carter a job and to stay with them until they could find an apartment. But the promised job disappeared, and they were evicted from their relatives' apartment by the landlord because there were too many of them living together. "When we first made the decision to move out here, we thought they were still in their home, they had previously owned a home; but they had moved from there, lost a home and moved to an apartment." The Carters then were forced to apply for welfare, and they found themselves unable to find another place to live, apparently because of having so many children.

Before finding the shelter, they slept in a car for one night, and then with another relative (who lived elsewhere in the area), where fourteen people were in one apartment for a night. They then received some emergency money and stayed in a hotel, in one room with a double bed for all six of them.

In Alabama they had owned a home, and Mr. Carter had had a steady job working in the security field. Suffering from too much stress, he started another job but was soon laid off. Meanwhile, Mrs. Carter was working part-time in minimum-wage nurses' aide positions, and her earnings did not even pay their mortgage. After Mr. Carter spoke with his relatives in California, they decided to make the change, since their options looked fairly bleak. Mrs. Carter explained,

> They had been telling us about, you could get a decent job, if you worked you could make it, and so I just told him one day, "I'd rather go to California than to stay here and not make it," because . . . we'd wind up with his mother or with my mother, and I didn't want to go back. . . . I got me a husband and four kids, and I got to go back home? . . . With the money we had saved up, because we sold our furniture and kids' clothes and all that stuff, to come out so we'd have enough to get started.

Mrs. Carter remembers her childhood in positive terms. Born thirty-three years ago, she grew up with her seven siblings and a grandparent in a home owned by her parents. Her father was a carpenter, her mother a nurse, and they apparently were able to provide quite well for their large family. "We always had a decent living, we never went lacking for anything. Our needs were met." She graduated from high school and spent two years in a technical college, taking psychology courses. Suddenly, her oldest sister died, and Mrs. Carter's life seemed to fall apart. "My outlook on life, I just let it go."

This event seems to have been a major turning point for her. Soon after, she had her first child (with another man) and began using drugs and alcohol. The man was violent with her occasionally, leading her to throw him out of the house at one point. She finally left him, met her present husband, and lived a relatively stable life with him for several years. She stopped using drugs and alcohol when her son was old enough to notice what she was doing. She is very concerned about trying to "be the mother that I've always knew my mother to be."

Mrs. Carter attributes most of their housing problems to the difficulty of finding affordable apartments for a family with four children. She says they have found places they could afford, but no one will rent to a family their size. She is quite optimistic about the future, however; she wants to complete her nursing training and become a physician's assistant, and Mr. Carter wants to start his own business. She even talks extensively of wanting to be in a position to "help people out," seeing herself in ten years as an "entrepreneur, where people say, 'Can you help *me* out?'"

Once again, we find ourselves struggling with the complex mixture of social pressures, blind chance, and individual decisions and habits that moved a person into homelessness. We might be more sympathetic about the bad luck and uncontrolled reasons for Mrs. Carter's problem, but the story shares with the earlier ones the ring of truth as it describes a life enmeshed in the simultaneous realities of control and noncontrol, of luck and responsibility. Even Mary Carter can look back at her life and regret certain decisions and patterns, even while she sees herself as having been victimized by both people and situations.

Who Are the Homeless?

It is apparent from the foregoing portraits that homeless families are not all alike. The circumstances that lead them to become homeless and their attitudes toward their situation vary dramatically. Stereotyping the homeless is as potentially dehumanizing and prejudicial as labeling any social group.

The romanticized portrait of the "worthy homeless" is an image that is not without some counterpart in shelters. Some families have fallen into poverty because of a single debilitating blow, such as a divorce that left the mother and children without any form of support. But others are families in which poverty runs several generations deep. Their movement into homelessness was not a fall so much as a side-step. The likelihood of these individuals ever making it into the middle class is remote.

Can the homeless be blamed for their condition? In many instances the precipitating factor is poor planning or judgment. But one has to ask also about cycles of poverty, the debilitating effects of childhood abuse, the reasons for mind-numbing drug and alcohol use, and the dilemma of providing shelter in the face of a housing shortage. What is cause? And what is effect?

Central to our concern in this book is whether the "worthy homeless" are the only ones deserving to be treated with dignity. Is the virtuous middle-class mother whose husband abandoned her the only one we respect, since we can identify personally with her plight? Or are all persons—alcoholics, drug abusers, and those who never learned the Protestant work ethic—to be treated with dignity? These are not insignificant questions because our answers to them powerfully affect the responses we—as individuals, as social institutions, and as a culture—make to homeless people.

PART TWO

Mediators of
Dignity

3

The Welfare System

Darlene Martin represents a very common pattern among people on welfare: she is a young black single mother with no job skills who became pregnant when she was seventeen and has been dependent on either husbands or welfare for most of her life. Although her parents divorced when she was young and had some money problems, she went through a relatively stable period with one of her husbands, owning a home in the southwestern United States. She reports that her two marriages failed because her husbands were not interested in being responsible fathers, and she had to be the one to raise the children and "give them the best. And this is what I'm striving toward, to give my kids the best."

She was living in the shelter with her two older children, hoping to pull herself out of the situation that had developed several months before when she was unable to pay the rent on her apartment. She then moved to a hotel that charged more money than she could afford, and finally she found herself without a place to live. She says that she has been unable to work because of the lack of child care, and she was unable to find the sort of minimum-wage jobs she was qualified for.

Her experiences with the welfare system are almost all negative, and they reflect many of the attitudes and responses people have to the institution that provides them with their food and shelter. She speaks first of the difficulty of surviving on welfare payments. "In one sense it was like an endless thing because of the fact, once you're in a hotel, it's like all the money that you get, and the County, it goes to the hotel, and then you doesn't get enough food stamps to cover just basically the thirty days." She has been unable to save any money when she lived in cheap hotels or apartments, and she complains that she found herself out on the street when one of her welfare checks didn't arrive on time.

Ms. Martin is particularly upset about the way she has been treated by the welfare system. She believes that "some of the [welfare] workers have a stigma against people being on AFDC, and they sort of let their frustrations out through things that they can have charge over. . . . I feel that's a prejudice against the person, and you're only hurting society because you are being able to cause a standstill in their life." She says that the vast majority of workers have this attitude. One worker insisted that she had to help herself and refused to do anything to assist her. She responded by reasserting her own sense of independence and dignity. "I thought like, I'm a grown person and I can be treated as an adult, and I'm going to respect you, and I would like for you to respect me, and just because I'm in this situation, this is not the way I'm planning on staying. . . . Your job is to serve people, and if you don't like to serve people, then you should find another profession."

Ms. Martin's perceptions of welfare workers mirror the way she feels treated by virtually everyone she comes in contact with. She is viewed purely externally, with no concern for her motives, her desires, or the reasons she is homeless. "They deal with the outside, but they don't deal with the inside," she complains, and the inside, for her, includes all the complexities of child care, transportation, and personal history that made her homeless—and that make it more difficult for her to escape from her present situation. Her life, in short, is more complicated than her welfare worker recognizes. "It's a lot of things inside of the picture book, but they look outside and they judge from the outside of it, and I think it makes it more harder on the person."

Her perceptions of how she is treated reveal many of the ways in which this social system undercuts the dignity of the individual. The system makes a typical set of assumptions about the persons it is supposed to serve: that they are on drugs, that they are not trying, that they expect handouts. And then the system also tends to focus on the "outside" rather than on the "inside"—to define persons by their present work or living situation, rather than assuming that an autonomous and responsible agent exists despite the present predicament.

Ms. Martin has also found little help from other assistance programs. She has attempted to find low-cost housing by applying for a special program that has "two or three years waiting lists, and the housing situation, everything is packed, just jam-packed." She believes that being on welfare is an added hindrance to finding an apartment because "people have a stigma against AFDC people, and even to get into regular housing, it's hard . . . to get low-income housing, but then you go apply for regular housing . . . and they turn you down. Even if you have the money, they'll turn you down." This perception makes it more difficult to persevere in trying to learn how to "work the system," since a kind of helplessness and despair sets in.

Ms. Martin believes that most people would be willing to help themselves if the government would provide the necessities such as education, child care, and information. "I believe, the ones that wants to know, if there was an opportunity . . . they would take advantage of it . . . instead of having AFDC, if someone wants to work. But when there's no openings, people just settle for what they are doing [by remaining on welfare]."

The Welfare System

The most significant source of intervention in the lives of homeless people is the welfare office, yet more than one in three of those we interviewed (thirty-nine people) indicated that they had experienced significant difficulties in dealing with this public agency whose mission is to assist the poor. A message echoing through our interviews is that you must first be humiliated or brutalized by the welfare system before public money can be given to you if you are homeless.

At the outset we must point to the danger of simply blaming the welfare workers or managers for the ways in which homeless families are treated. There is certainly enough deserved blame of this sort to go around, and there are valid concerns about unfair or impersonal treatment of clients, reports of which we heard repeatedly. But many of these problems are systemic; the welfare worker's job is usually an unenviable one, with enormous pressures and poor working conditions. In discussing the problems from the viewpoint of the homeless families, we are not assuming that most welfare workers are inherently insensitive or malicious.

The ritual of humiliation often begins with the determination of one's eligibility. The questions about eligibility for welfare programs are complicated. The eligibility rules and the ways in which people are accepted or rejected are hard to understand, a fact that undermines a sense of control or predictability for homeless families. For example, one controversy concerns whether people are required to verify that they are homeless in order to receive their special homeless assistance grant from the county. Our attempts to resolve the disagreement by speaking to people within the welfare system met with a similar degree of confusion, and no one has a clear answer.

It is likely that much of the uncertainty is intentional, allowing the eligibility workers to hide behind the requirement of verification while giving them flexibility when they choose to use it. The net result, however, appears to be that people who are more insistent, or who have someone knowledgeable about the rules (such as a shelter advocate) intervening for them, can receive the money without providing any proof, while the less knowledgeable or more passive people are more likely to be deterred from pursuing the benefits they may be entitled to.

It is reasonable to expect the social service system to seek verification from people who receive benefits. After all, tax money is being spent, and anecdotal stories of welfare cheats cannot be dismissed as pure hyperbole. However, it is important to recognize the extent to which the system seems to reinforce the view that welfare recipients are untrustworthy and lazy. The insensitivity of the system creates many of the problems. For example, although it is reasonable to try to assure that someone is homeless before receiving certain funds, we heard numerous accounts of staff workers who simply failed to understand how hard (if not impossible) it may be to prove.

Similarly, it was pointed out that the welfare system has elaborate controls to prevent overpayments, but none to control underpayments or late payments. When there is confusion over a policy (such as requiring people to prove they are homeless), workers are more likely to err on the side of withholding assistance, for fear of being reprimanded. The underlying mentality of the system is revealed in the fact that the Los Angeles welfare department referred to its staff members as "eligibility workers," stressing their role as gatekeepers rather than helpers.

Other features of eligibility rules are particularly relevant for understanding how the system undermines personal dignity. For example, families are ineligible to receive AFDC if a parent works more than one hundred hours a month. Such a limitation may be understandable politically, but it only serves to create the image that full-time work is a threat to (rather than a release from) one's present status. Such a limitation also is unreasonable in terms of the actual incomes most people in this population are able to make versus the expenses necessary to support their families.

Problems for immigrants are even greater. Several people have been unable to receive any assistance because they have no green cards, and language barriers are severe in many instances. Many shelters do not have staff members who speak Spanish, so the available facilities are more limited; the same problems are encountered in the welfare system, particularly by people who are afraid of their marginal or illegal immigrant status.

One theme heard commonly in comments about both the shelters and the welfare system is the importance of having a person to help you negotiate the process. One woman was repeatedly frustrated by rejections from workers at shelters and at the welfare office. People hung up the phone in the middle of conversations, and she felt convinced that "nobody wants to talk to you. . . . I might as well be talking to myself." She is furious "because there are so many organizations and people who are supposed to help you." "When it comes down to it, nobody wants to do anything for you unless you have an advocate or somebody that's really going to say, 'Hey, this is against the law what you're doing to this person.' . . . Because you can't do anything by yourself, it seems like nobody wants to speak to you."

Then this woman met a staff worker at one shelter and suddenly "it was like magic. She opened doors. . . . It was like the Lord speaking, they had to do what she said, it was magic. I couldn't believe it." She points up the

importance of having such an advocate. "Now if people could know somebody like Sister Kathleen or somebody who was willing to speak for them and
stand behind them, it makes things a *lot* easier. . . . It makes a big difference."

There is a certain irony in only being able to find such an advocate when
you are already homeless. The obvious question is why this could not have
happened earlier. One woman speaks for many others when she remembers
how hard it was to receive any help from AFDC when she was trying
desperately to make ends meet in her last apartment, and how much easier
things have been since she became homeless. The conclusion she draws is
somewhat chilling, albeit logical: she is better off saving a month's rent and
becoming homeless in order to receive more assistance later. She recognizes
the absurdity of the situation: "Why do I have to become homeless to get the
help? If I can get the help, if I screw up and I make myself look like a jerk and
I'm homeless, then I can get help!"

Instead of receiving small amounts of help when something goes wrong,
she feels the system forces her to wait until she is desperate. "You've gotta trip
yourself up and become homeless in order to get the money to do that. You
have to make yourself look almost irresponsible." She told us that her case
workers look at her like she's crazy if she says she wants to get off welfare.
After all, the system seems to her to be designed to perpetuate dependence
and a cycle of poverty that drives people into a state of need for which more
funding will be available.

From the perspective of the person enmeshed in such a system, the
message seems clear. It is as if the support networks do not know how to deal
with someone who is partially independent or partially disabled. You are
either a fully responsible adult, in which case we will treat you with dignity; or
you are helpless and in need, in which case we will give you assistance but in a
manner and with conditions that assume that you are no longer a functioning
responsible adult.

We believe that the system's inability to deal with the grey areas in which
people find themselves merely mirrors the everyday problem we face in
dealing with homeless people confronting us on the streets. In deciding how
to view the homeless, how many of us are able to find an alternative between
dismissing them as lazy or pitying them as helpless? We should not be
surprised that our social systems are no better able to avoid either/or interpretations in responding to these complex and troubled lives.

The Experience of Welfare

The clearest way to capture the gritty experience of a welfare office is to
visit one. We spent an afternoon in one of the offices where many of the
shelter residents go every week or two to receive their checks, to reapply for

benefits, or to try to clear up problems they have encountered. The visit occurred in the middle of a month, so the caseload was fairly typical. The welfare office consisted of two extremely large and crowded rooms, each with connected rows of uncomfortable plastic chairs. The walls were bare except for numerous sheets of paper detailing rules and procedures to be followed in applying for and retaining welfare benefits.

There were almost one hundred people in the main waiting room, including many young children running around and crying; most people had at least one child with them. The chairs faced a set of windows at the front, behind which a few staffers answered questions. Across the hall was another large room for medical aid and other programs, and that room was even more crowded.

The time passed very slowly. Approximately once or twice each hour, a staff member appeared from the back room and called out someone's name; otherwise, people just sat, staring straight ahead or trying to keep their children from intruding on the strangers surrounding them. The fact that the one clock on the wall was one hour slow seemed to represent both the pace of the enterprise and the lack of concern about the people who were waiting.

We can report similar impressions in our various attempts to gather information or set up appointments with people in the welfare system. For example, a conversation with a representative of one of the major homeless assistance programs revealed that the person had little knowledge of the details of the program. We could only try to imagine what the experience would be like for a frightened and uneducated person trying to get the same information.

The inefficiency of the welfare system is all too well known, and the interviews we recorded revealed the standard range of problems. In particular, as a homeless advocate also pointed out, unexplained failure to receive a check on time is a significant cause of homelessness, and the legal aid organization in Los Angeles has even set up a special lock-out clinic to deal with this growing problem. In 1986 a Superior Court judge referred to the application procedures for general relief as "a massive bureaucracy. . . . I don't understand some of the forms myself." According to a *Los Angeles Times* editorial, a homeless person able to work has to complete a form with twenty addresses, phone numbers, and signatures of potential employers in order to receive certain types of assistance.[1]

The system often works as humanely as it does only because of intervention from advocacy lawyers. For example, in 1986 legal aid lawyers forced the state welfare office to reverse a policy that removed children from their homeless parents if the parents requested food or emergency shelter from the government.[2] Other rules also make it extremely difficult for people to deal in an organized and planned way with their financial crises. For example, no landlord-tenant rights exist for people who stay in motels for less than thirty days, and many managers give only thirty-day leases as a result. Such policies mitigate against the homeless being able to make long-range plans or to be protected from a sudden eviction.

Dealing with the welfare system is one of the major sources of disaffection and frustration for the homeless shelter residents who participated in our study. We heard various stories. One man complained that he was kicked off of AFDC because he didn't know his son's mother's social security number or where she was living at the time. Another woman was unable to receive her welfare checks because she didn't have an address, and the office refused to count the shelter as her place of residence. Some people complained that their children were almost taken away from them because they were homeless, especially in other localities.

A pregnant woman was denied welfare assistance for her other children for a few weeks and is frustrated about the delay and the procedures. She reports that "they give you the runaround, they want to see the kids, they want a birth certificate, they want this, they want that, they want everything from you. And then they say, 'Well, I don't know if I can give you the money today.'" She is particularly upset at the grudging way in which the assistance is provided and the assumption that people enjoy asking for handouts. "They act like they're taking the money out of their pockets. . . . They say, 'We have to screen people who get on AFDC, because a lot of people try to get on AFDC and they have jobs already.' I said, 'Nobody wants to come down here and deal with this if they have a job.'"

The unpredictability of dealing with the welfare system is often tied to the life-style and temperament of the individual. For example, a woman admits that she has had problems receiving her benefits regularly because "I couldn't remember all the time just to send [the forms] in on time . . . or I'd put it on the mailbox and it would blow away with the wind or something, and eventually I'd find out I'm cut off."

The attitudes of welfare workers are frequently criticized. People accused the welfare workers of disliking them personally and of singling them out for bad treatment. We heard comments that the workers were "spiteful," "coldhearted," or "prejudiced." Other people complain that they have been addressed curtly and angrily by workers asking them, "Why didn't you get a job?" Rules are often enforced rigidly: a woman laughed as she told us that she was required to provide proof of her pregnancy. "I was this big and I had to have proof! I said, 'Oh God, what's next?'" Another woman reports, "I've never had a case worker yet that has really cared [laughs]. 'Whatever you want to do, fine.' . . . It's like they have so much to do that everything is always so mixed up, and you're always in limbo." A woman complains that the welfare worker makes her feel like "it's *her* money that she's giving you. This is the way they feel, make you feel anyway. If they can cut down on giving you anything."

Of course, there is no way to determine with certainty whether these accounts are accurate or whether there were other reasons for the problems these people encountered. What is certain, however, is that the subjective experience of dealing with the welfare office often involves a series of hassles, unintelligible rules, insensitive workers, and unpredictable delays.

As we mentioned earlier, it would be too easy to blame welfare personnel or the social service system itself for all of these problems. Caseloads have increased dramatically in the past few years, workers are overworked and undertrained, and the entire system is forced politically into a budget-driven and adversarial approach to its clientele. We occasionally heard a recognition of the difficult task facing the welfare workers and heard suggestions about how to improve communication and openness. One woman commented that the welfare office "was understaffed, the place is just booked solid, and those people, the social workers, they look like they were just totally exhausted." It is clear that many of the rules (such as the hours offices are open and the application and reapplication procedures) are greater hindrances than the personal attitudes or style of the workers themselves.

In addition, it should be noted that some people are quite willing to take responsibility for the problems they have had with the welfare system. One woman was required to reapply for a housing program when she moved, but she told us that she had to do so "because I had moved too much, it had served me right for doing that."

The general frustration at the system's inability to treat people with dignity is represented in the following comments by a very angry woman: "The worst is AFDC. I went to them and told them, 'Hey, I have no place to go, I am homeless with two children.' They tell me, 'You should have gotten here earlier.' I asked them, 'Okay, I should have gotten here earlier, but I didn't. I still need the same assistance. I'm still homeless.'" This same woman is also furious because she arrived late at a welfare office and was denied help. When told there was nothing they could do to help her, she responded, "Is there a special time you have to become homeless? Do I have to be homeless between nine and two?"

There is little doubt that people who are in trouble can learn how to "work the system" and that many homeless people become quite adept in doing so. Because our interviews were conducted in the shelters, we would expect people to be quite hesitant about admitting to such maneuvers. But we did hear several stories of people who had worked illegally to make some extra money. The same woman just quoted provided a fascinating rationale for her ability to work the system against its own rules.

I was saving money a little at a time to get an apartment. But then the checks—what I was doing, and I'm going to be honest with you, I was working dishonestly, maybe this is why a lot of things happened. I did not tell welfare I was working, simply because I did not want them to cut my check. . . . I told my worker, "If I find a job, I'm going to work, I'm not going to tell you a damn thing. Catch me, I'll pay it back. I'm just that angry. Catch me!"

She says that she has asked for help without any effect and insists that she deserves the assistance, in part because of her own work history. "I don't feel that I'm taking anything or I'm sitting on my ass and not working. I worked for over twenty years, and each check gave money for AFDC. I feel as though I have just put money in the bank, and right now I'm drawing interest off of it. . . . I do not intend to be a AFDC recipient the rest of my life. As a matter of fact, I won't be one by the end of the year."

Her anger at the system involves many of the other elements we have already identified. She was told that she was not supposed to be married and have her husband living with her, to which she retorted, "So what do I do with him, throw him away? . . . They force the man out of the household, but they're supposed to be assisting you." And her experience with being denied help when she arrived after working hours leaves her wondering whether the system cares at all about either her or her children. "Life is not supposed to be fair, but I'm saying, give the children a better chance, it is not their fault. It is not *my* fault I'm homeless."

Benefits and Needs

The benefits provided by welfare programs are scarcely sufficient to provide even the temporary and limited assistance for which they are designed. A 1988 study by an advocacy group reported that "the average value of AFDC benefits fell by 35 percent [from 1970 to 1987], to only 44.2 percent of the federal poverty level. In 41 states, the combined value of AFDC and Food Stamps is less than 75 percent of the poverty level."[3]

Nevertheless, the current welfare system has some very valuable features. Among the many programs that are most helpful is the Women, Infants, and Children (WIC) program, which provides supplemental food, education, and counseling for pregnant women and mothers with very young children. A woman acknowledges that Los Angeles provides better welfare benefits than the smaller town in the Midwest she used to live in. "I feel these people have been better to me, and me being an outsider, than what my home town would have done for me, mainly because they don't have the money as much as they do here, and then the population here is so much larger too. You've got a little more people that can help you a little more than what they can in Ohio."

But there is a widespread perception that the welfare system does not provide sufficient financial assistance to help people out in any significant way. Several people told us that they had virtually no money left over after paying their rent, even with AFDC support for several children. One woman complains that she is constantly told to look for a place to live but finds it a fruitless endeavor: "What for? It's a waste of time and energy. I haven't had any money to get a place if I found it." Recognizing that welfare is "a dead-end street," she wants to find a job and support herself but feels trapped because she cannot save enough money to get started.

In another case, a woman says that she was unable to keep her apartment on the five hundred dollars she was receiving. She does not want to be on welfare, she insists, and reports that she would spend most of her paycheck simply providing decent baby-sitting care for her children. The housing market makes it impossible for her to live on what she is receiving, and she cannot find a place in any of the HUD projects or Section 8 housing units that are supposed to be available. But she is continually confronted by people who accuse her of "sitting home collecting AFDC," prompting her to respond, "Well, if I'm out, I'm spending money, on the bus, or the kids see stuff, and you can't always tell them no. . . . And then it's a domino factor, where you've taken X, Y, and Z from rent money . . . and then you can't catch up. . . . It's like there's no safety net."

In some cases it is the insensitivity and ignorance of the welfare workers that is the most troubling aspect of the financial limitations. One woman reports that her worker told her that she had to find a permanent place to live with the $210 she was receiving as her only financial assistance. "That's absolutely ridiculous!" A man was asked by his social worker whether he was looking for a permanent place to stay. "I said, with what? You show me a landlord that'll let me move in without a red cent, and I'll be there in a flash. . . . It's so illogical. Have you been searching? It's ludicrous."

Another woman states the financial problem even more directly. "Give us some more money, because we need more money. Because you can't work and get your checks, because they take whatever you make, they take off your check. So what's the difference working, if they're going to do that? You're trying to earn extra money because you're out there working, why they still going to take it?"

Welfare: Stereotypes and Realities

We heard a number of comments that undermine the stereotype of welfare recipients as people who love to take advantage of handouts. A married woman is trying to solve her present problems without returning to dependence on the welfare system. "I don't want to go back on welfare—is that so wrong, even though I'm homeless? I've been on it for almost ten years, I'm tired of it, I want my husband and me to work. I don't want to be on welfare no more. They keep telling me in here I have to go apply for AFDC. I don't want to."

A married man points out that the social system seems to run on precisely the stability and proof of security that homeless people do not possess.

A person who's homeless, sometimes one of your major problems is you have lost those little handholds that allow you to be a part of society, and that is picture identification, security cards. And it costs you money to get those.... General relief will help you get an I.D. only if you've never had an I.D. here! ... Everybody can count you as a nonentity not to be helped if you don't have identification.... The people who usually benefit from most of these programs are usually crooked people [because they can get fake identification].

Like the woman quoted earlier, he is particularly resentful of the welfare system for treating him like an outcast rather than recognizing that he has been a productive member of society. He is angry, he says, "because I've always worked and I've paid my taxes when I was supposed to, and I feel really cheated. If I'd kept the money I'd paid out in taxes, I'd have it." This comment provides a powerful vision of what our society seems to have lost—the communal sense of "being in it together," a shared trust that all citizens deserve to be helped when they have problems because they can be trusted to help when they do not.

The impersonality of the system further undermines the sense of self-worth for homeless people. One woman angrily told us: "I could talk until I'm blue in the face and it wouldn't do me any good, none.... I'd be so frustrated, I'd be talking to them on the telephone and they'd just put the phone down, they don't hang up, they just put the phone down."

The requirement for identification and credit simply makes the situation worse. Another woman has been having serious problems finding an apartment because "I don't have no papers. They asked me for a social security number.... [They] wouldn't take me because they didn't have no reference or anything, or credit."

Finally, it is important to notice that many people on welfare themselves recognize the hazards of the program and the dangers of becoming too dependent. Indeed, they often blame the system for making it so difficult to escape from the cycle of poverty and homelessness. One woman is terrified about this possibility. "You get stuck in a rut, and you can't get off, they won't let you get off, and if you do try, they punish you, and that's the bad part of welfare.... Welfare is a beautiful thing, it's not a way of life.... Instead of keeping [people] behind, let them get ahead. If they get a job, let them have that little extra money for a couple of months. It'll pay off in the long run." In other words, far from taking advantage of the system's benefits, she is suggesting that the rules make it more difficult to escape from the dependence fostered by welfare itself. She is afraid of the tendency of the system to make the person afraid to try to get off, for fear of being cut off completely from any assistance or support.

We do a terrible injustice to people on welfare if we assume that most of them are manipulative or lazy. It is evident that many people recognize full well the disadvantages of the welfare system and that most of them would like to find jobs and living conditions that would enable them to rely on their own paychecks. There may be people who would prefer to remain on welfare rather than finding a job. But the reality for most of our homeless families makes such a choice irrelevant: the jobs they are likely to find would not enable them to find and afford apartments in which they could provide security or safety for their children. In interpreting their continued reliance on a system that continues to infantilize and debilitate them, we are forced to remind ourselves of their actual alternatives, given both their lack of job training and the emotional and psychological scars from their recent experiences.

Dignity and the Welfare System

The central issue in addressing the relationship between the welfare system and personal dignity is the attitude that we as a society have toward the poor. Financial common sense seems to require that a distinction be made between the deserving and nondeserving poor. Americans cannot be criticized for not wanting tax money spent on people who are simply taking advantage of the system. But to phrase the choice in such terms overstates the facts. There is little doubt that most people receiving welfare would rather be living different sorts of lives, and most of them have little choice, given their present level of family responsibilities, job training, available income, and the lack of alternative housing and employment opportunities.

In addition, we must ask whether the process of making such distinctions need involve humiliating the applicant. Need the "deserving" poor be subjected to ritual humiliation as a condition of ongoing assistance? Our society has an obligation to determine who should be assisted by welfare without dehumanizing the applicant, and it is morally wrong to continually haze those who society has determined *are* eligible.

In making this judgment, we are not addressing the issue of who should be eligible and what the level of payment should be. All human beings should be treated with dignity, whether they are poor or wealthy. While prejudice against people of color has finally become an issue for open discussion, no similar awareness exists of prejudice against the poor. There may be limits to what any society can do in creating a safety net for the poor, but humiliation should not be a condition of providing services and support to the needy members of society.

Analogies can provide images for understanding the possibility of welfare and personal dignity existing side-by-side. Eligibility determinations are made regularly in our society in other areas of social life without humiliating the applicant. For example, students and their parents apply for scholarship assistance. They supply detailed financial information, but a determination is made without attacking the self-respect of the applicant. Likewise, banks continually deal with applications for loans and credit cards. Careful judgments have to be made about who qualifies, but the bank that routinely humiliated its customers would not survive for long.

The dignity of homeless persons has already been attacked by the mere fact that they are, for the moment, dependent and in need of help. At these moments, homeless families, in particular, need to be treated with the courtesy that builds, rather than undermines, their self-respect. No public system or institution has the right to denigrate those it is supposed to assist.

But the treatment of homeless persons by the welfare system raises larger issues of how our society views them. As we have noted, the welfare workers are our representatives; to criticize them for humiliating or insulting people is to acknowledge our own complicity. The issue turns once again to how we treat the most vulnerable in our midst, and to whether the meager survival mechanisms we provide will uphold or undermine their dignity.

We would suggest that the entire structure of dispensing welfare makes it extremely difficult to maintain a sense of dignity for the adult "recipients." To highlight the structures we take for granted, it may be helpful to point to a very different way of providing for the needs of the poor in the past. This is a model that may not be practical today but serves to remind us of the problems we have created.

In the Bible farmers were expected to leave one portion of their fields for the poor: "When you reap the harvest of your land, you shall not reap your field to its very border, neither shall you gather the gleanings after your harvest. And you shall not strip your vineyard bare, neither shall you gather the fallen grapes of your vineyard; you shall leave them for the poor and for the sojourner" (Leviticus 19:9–10; cf. Deuteronomy 24:19–22).

Consider the logistics of such an arrangement. There is no handout, no direct giving and taking, no embarrassed looks and side-glances. Indeed, the giver does not know who receives, and the receiver does not know who gives.[4] The understanding is that the "leavings" are the rightful possession of the poor and the sojourner—not by the grace of the giver, but simply in the order of things. In avoiding the direct confrontation, and in providing rules for a more passive exchange, the biblical model points to some of the dangers of our present system.

We appear to be stuck with our present system, and there may be no way to avoid the interpersonal tension and hostility it engenders. But we can remind ourselves of our responsibility to ensure that welfare is viewed not as gift but as necessary support, and that the person receiving assistance remains a person to be treated with dignity.

4

Shelters

Fred Barton is a fifty-year-old black man, raising his six-year-old son James, whose mother left them soon after the child was born. Mr. Barton and James had been "going from motel to hotel, and shelter to shelter" for quite a while before ending up in the shelter where Mr. Barton was interviewed.

Fred Barton grew up in the projects of a large eastern city. Although he says that he was a good student, he left school when he was sixteen and joined the army, after which he went to work in the steel mills. After steady work for over twenty years, the mills closed, and he decided to move to California to make a fresh start. He worked for several years in the mills until he was laid off after injuring his back at work. He and his new wife and young child lived for a while on the disability settlement he received, but when the money ran out his wife left them.

His experiences since running out of money read almost like a travelogue of the options open to homeless families. He and his son lived in a mission in Los Angeles, a city park, several hotels and motels, and a number of different types of shelters. He recounted a series of horrible experiences, including a violent fight with someone in one of the hotels and a series of dangerous encounters at other facilities. But he continued to try to find some institutional setting, in part because of a terrifying experience that happened when they were camping out at a large public encampment called "Tent City." "We went there one time," he said. "This guy was nice enough to give us a sleeping bag and let us stay in his little tent thing. And the next morning we woke up, and my son's face was all swoll up where the mosquitos had bitten, and that scared me to death. And I thought, right now I'll kill to get inside, to get him out of these streets.... That was the scariest time of our being homeless. It hurt me real bad, because he was disfigured, he was disfigured, I'm telling you."

On two separate occasions when Mr. Barton was standing in food lines with his son, they saw violent stabbings occur right in front of them. He was very concerned about the effect these events will have on James, and he became even more convinced that he must find a place to stay.

But his experiences in some of the shelters were not much better. They stayed in one facility where they were forced to sleep on cots next to a woman who had insects crawling all over her body. "I tell the guy, 'We can't stay here, look at this lady! Do something for her! Well, she's right next to my son.' . . . They called somebody, but they let her stay there. . . . we had to move our cots way over in the corner somewhere to get away from this." They stayed in another religiously affiliated shelter which, he notes, "has been closed down three times that I know for epidemic, one time epidemic of hepatitis, once for pneumonia, and once for the flu. That's scary. . . . I guess that's about the worst place I've ever been in, other than Tent City." Yet another shelter was filled with drug addicts and alcoholics.

He is convinced that "somehow it wears on the kids, it comes off on the kids." "I can see his intelligence dropping, I can see the change in him. . . . He was trying to act like the other kids, the other kids were acting real wild, and he's just kind of changing his whole personality, and it bothered me. Just like now, it's going to change for the worst if I stay down here." Although Mr. Barton can recognize the advantages of staying in a shelter that allows him to save money and at least provides a place for his son to sleep off the streets, he remains nervous and frustrated about the ways in which no institutional shelter can truly provide the secure emotional shelter he so deeply desires for himself and his son.

The Shelters

Our interviews were conducted in five shelters in the Los Angeles area. To provide some sense of the situations in which our interviewees found themselves, we offer a brief description of the shelters here.

Forty interviews were done in a large shelter that consisted of a two-story apartment building, where residents lived, and a house that served as an office. This shelter differed from the others in that residents had their own private apartments, with bath and kitchen. Residents could lock their doors, and there were no rules regarding curfews or leaving the shelter during the day. As a result, residents shared child care and came and went as one might in a typical apartment setting. The shelter was service-intensive, providing psychological counseling as well as parent effectiveness classes. Staff informed us that they only admitted families that they believed had a high probability of functioning independently after leaving the shelter. As in all the shelters where we conducted interviews, alcohol and drugs were strictly forbidden on the premises.

Twenty-two interviews were conducted in a twelve-family shelter with a more "homey feeling." It was located in a residential neighborhood and previously had been an apartment building. Each family had one or two rooms, depending on the size of the family, that were connected to a private bath and kitchen shared with one other room. Residents cooked their own food and had a significant degree of autonomy over their daily schedules. However, the interviewees voiced strong resentment over the requirement that residents leave the shelter during the day. Every morning there was a group meeting of adult residents and social workers. These meetings lasted thirty minutes to an hour and focused on issues involved with living together. Sometimes these meetings were very perfunctory, and sometimes they were very intense—especially if there had been a problem with theft or some other issue that threatened living together.

Nineteen of the interviews were conducted at a multistory shelter that had a very institutional character, with a reception desk and office on the lower floor and residents' rooms on the upper floors. Residents each had their own separate room, although there were regulations against locking one's door. Meals were served by shelter staff in a cafeteria-style lunchroom. Residents had to observe a strict curfew, and they were asked to leave if they had several infractions. There was very limited child care except, for example, when a resident had an appointment with a shelter counselor; otherwise residents had to stay with their children. Rules prohibited leaving children with another resident, and older children were not allowed to baby-sit for younger children. In general, the shelter was fairly bureaucratically organized, with rules that made it difficult to search for a job, look for housing, or go to the welfare office.

Ten interviews were done in another institutional-type setting. This shelter was in a badly deteriorating neighborhood, and interviewees often mentioned that it was not safe to be out at night there. The shelter had many rules and required residents to leave during the day as well as return by a specific curfew time. Meals were served cafeteria style at established times. There were considerable complaints about the food, the staff, and the rules of the shelter. Residents were required to sign up for specific chores as part of their contract for staying at the shelter. Limited child care was provided for residents if they were seeing a staff member or having a job interview.

Finally, nine interviews were conducted in a smaller, woman-only institutional shelter that, from the exterior, appeared to be a house. Offices, a large playroom, and the kitchen occupied the ground floor. Upstairs there were four or five rooms for residents and their children, all of whom shared the same large bath. The relationship between residents and staff was very friendly. Residents were allowed to stay in the shelter during the day, and they prepared meals together in the large shared kitchen. This shelter had a reputation for taking women and children who might not be admitted to more selective shelters (for example, undocumented workers, lesbians, and so on).

Discovering Shelter

Who actually goes to the shelters? It has been suggested that newly homeless people are more likely to bypass the shelters and use their homeless assistance money to stay in a motel. Because the government assistance is not sufficient to help the most needy, shelters are becoming more likely to dredge the ranks of the homeless rather than to skim off the very best and most successful people.[1] But shelters differ dramatically on this point; indeed, our five shelters are among the few that are still able to attract the best by setting fairly high standards for admission.

It is ironic that the very people who most need the benefits of the shelter environment may be the ones who are least likely to be there. The shelters that provide the best living conditions and the most thorough services are likely to be the same ones that are quite selective in who they take in, and it is the families with severe problems or coping limitations that are most likely to be left out. The shelters argue, of course, that they must try to provide their limited services to those who can most benefit from them—the result is a triage system for the provision of beds, food, and social services.

In addition, the qualities required to take advantage of the time in a shelter are likely to be those that these people lack. For example, a passive attitude resulting from months of homelessness makes a person less able to use the shelter system to best advantage. One resident pointed this out by saying,

> I think to get out of this situation. . . . what a person has to do is take advantage of every opportunity while they're here, and be pushy and mad. Because the workers here, when they interview you, they give you certain specific rules which aren't bad, and that's fine, but they give you the idea that they are going to be working with you. They're limited too, and it's up to you to push them, to say "I want to use the phone, you said that I could use the phone." I think you have to really, really push.

The resulting situation is often self-defeating. Shelters exist to help those who become homeless, and those who become homeless are likely to experience their lives in passive and unpredictable terms. Yet to make the most of the shelter experience, a more active and self-affirming stance is necessary, particularly because of the short-term nature of the residence system. How likely am I to "really, really push," when my recent life has been a series of events that have undermined my belief that I can affect my social world in the first place?

The selection process of assigning people to shelters is often haphazard and demeaning. Because less than half of the people in Los Angeles can be placed in shelters on most nights, there is often an intermediary who tries to determine whether the person is "right" for the shelter, and vice versa.[2] In the process, of course, the underlying fact of the situation is pushed aside: namely, that this individual needs a place to stay, and the shelter has a bed to provide.

Even when shelters are available, people are often unwilling to stay in them. The reasons vary, including privacy, strict rules, pride, physical dangers, and insecurity.[3] One writer has captured the thoughts and feelings of people who might choose not to enter a shelter:

> The streets or parks have their own dangers . . . but they allow some measure of choice and of control over one's environment [compared to many shelters]. It is possible to choose one's place to sleep where it seems to be safest and to move away when danger appears to be imminent. One can also have a personal space and a measure of privacy that does not exist in many shelters. There is also proximity with other people who are not homeless in contrast with the ghetto-ized environment of the shelter, which results from the fact that all guests are homeless. Some people are unable to accept the regimentation and institutional aspects of some shelters. For these reasons, many people prefer the streets, parks, beaches, or public places to shelters.[4]

How does a person find a shelter? For our respondents, the most common route involved a recommendation or referral from a social service worker, either at another shelter or in a religious or service organization to which the person had turned for help. These workers are usually well acquainted with the range of shelters but are unable to match up people with the appropriate shelter because of the small number of vacancies. Therefore, most people are directed to a particular shelter after someone else has identified an opening in that facility.

Other people find a shelter through word of mouth or a notice on a food bank bulletin board. Because they do not have an intermediary to help them, these people are at a significant disadvantage, and often they must call upon their lobbying skills, their ability to elicit sympathy, and the good luck of showing up at a shelter just as someone else is leaving. One person spent over a week trying to locate an opening and called every day to determine who would be able to accommodate her family that night.

Once a shelter opening is found, other problems arise immediately. Because Los Angeles is so large, getting to the shelter is no easy task. Some people were forced to walk long distances, children and minimal possessions in hand, in order to arrive at the shelter before closing time. Most shelters do not admit new arrivals in the evenings or on weekends, so these people began their sojourn to the shelter at a frantic (and often panicked) pace to avoid finding themselves with no place to sleep that night.

Arriving at the shelter is usually traumatic, even if an opening has already been secured. In spite of the best efforts of shelter staff, these families are coming into a strange and frightening situation, exhausted (and often dirty) from their experiences of the previous few days and surrounded suddenly by people who may appear very different and even intimidating. The check-in areas of these shelters are often crowded and noisy; there are papers to be completed, questions to be answered, rules to be learned, and schedules to be followed. For a disoriented and depressed adult with small children, the first contact with the shelter is usually a very mixed blessing.

However, the other side of the story is equally important. People who arrive at these shelters have been living confusing and often terrifying lives in the immediate past. They have worried about whether they will be able to find a safe place for their children, and many of them are worried that they will actually have their children taken away from them by state authorities. They have usually been looking for a stable residence for days or weeks, often calling shelters to see if there are openings. They are almost always at the end of their rope, feeling abandoned by family, friends, and society.

In addition, picture their specific living conditions before entering the shelter. In the best of cases, they have been sleeping in small and dingy apartments or motels or sharing crowded living quarters with distant relatives or acquaintances. For others, the past weeks have involved sleeping in cars, on park benches, or on the beach, huddled together for warmth and afraid of being robbed or attacked by passersby. They have usually been bounced around from agency to agency, from advisor to advisor, with little time to reflect on what is happening and even less reason to believe that their situation will improve.

In this context, shelters are a welcome relief from the radical insecurity and terror. The sense of relief is reinforced by the often-friendly voices and faces of the shelter workers, who seem to try to make them feel as welcome as possible. The families arrive, bringing whatever belongings they may have dragged with them across the city, and are provided with necessities that most of us take for granted: a room, a bed, a shower, a meal. Most striking of all, they are told that they do not have to leave the next day; in most shelters in Los Angeles residents are allowed to stay for one or two months.

It would be hard to indicate how relieved and grateful these people are upon arriving at the shelter. However small their rooms and however limited their privacy, however patronizing and controlling the manner of their treatment, they have been taken into a place that is there for them, which promises to provide their children some respite from the streets, and which will allow them to stay for longer than a day or two. It is small wonder that the shelters are perceived as lifesavers and that these people are eager to stay as long as they can.

Arriving at a shelter represents both success and failure, however. Denial is no longer possible; like the alcoholic forced to stand up and confess "I am an alcoholic," each person now is homeless by definition, living in a shelter with other homeless people. In addition, however friendly and supportive the staff may be, they are explicitly caretakers, counselors, or custodians—people paid to look after, to provide assistance. No one can enter a shelter and fail to appreciate the striking loss of autonomy that suddenly becomes so apparent.

Life in the Shelter

As the residents settle in, they often begin to compare the shelters, not so much to the insecurity of their past few days but to their earlier, often more-settled lives. As a result, many aspects of shelter life begin to represent disappointments and threats to their dignity at the same time as the shelters provide a needed haven and social support.

In the five shelters we observed, the most important factors affecting the treatment of the residents stem from the physical and temporal realities of the facility. Space is at a premium, as it is in most apartments or motels poor people live in. Families are usually packed into one or two small rooms, often with bunk beds and virtually no extra floor space. Kitchen facilities are usually shared with other families, or meals are provided and served at set times by shelter staff.

Space is also limited in the rest of the building. There is seldom any place to go to sit and be alone or to carry on a private conversation. The effects of such living conditions on privacy and confidentiality are evident. For example, we observed an initial intake interview being conducted in an open public space between a staff member and a new resident, who was telling (in full hearing of anyone who passed by) her story of explicit sexual abuse of her children by relatives. Similarly, we overheard a rather violent argument between two mothers, one of whom was angry because her son had been physically disciplined by the other woman. The two had no place to go to carry on their argument, so other residents simply walked around them and tried to ignore the emotional exchange.

In addition to space, living conditions in most shelters provide little sense of comfort or "home." Most homeless facilities have an institutional feeling, which is a result of financial limitations and the large numbers of people being housed. Our experiences revealed that hallways are usually dreary, walls are bare and in need of paint, and the rooms consist of the bare minimum amount of creature comforts.

Living in close proximity with other homeless people creates tensions and problems. Parents have no control over the type of people who are affecting their children and have little if any influence over the ways in which the shelter is administered. In response, these people may try to shut themselves off from everyone around them in order to avoid "contaminating" themselves. A powerful statement of this response appeared in a newspaper article about a twelve-year-old boy who told a reporter that he "didn't want to be here, sharing the floor with grizzly men. 'Look at all the Skid Row bums. . . . It's dull and dumb and, if it was my world, I would set it on fire. . . . I feel like a dead cat.' "[5] Although the situation in our shelters was not this stark, the same sense of alienation and fear looms in the lives of people who no longer feel that they are living in a supportive or compatible environment.

Once again, however, we must always ask ourselves what the appropriate point of comparison is in assessing such facilities. As we indicated, for most residents the alternative was a sidewalk, a public park, a car, or a dingy and tiny motel room or shared apartment.[6] Compared to these options, shelters do provide some critical support for homeless families. In the midst of the criticisms and complaints, we heard much praise and thankfulness for the shelters.

Not surprisingly, the identified positive features are directly correlated with the ability of shelters to support the dignity of the homeless person. For example, a woman living with her husband and teenage son is grateful that the shelter provides opportunities and help for her in this unique situation in her life. She is pleased to be receiving food, clothing, a bed, and shower facilities. But equally important to her is the fact that "they allow you to feel that you are a human being, and that just because you've gotten into a bad situation . . . they're not constantly reminding you that you're here and why and you've put yourself in this situation and this is all you have to look forward to, you're never going to get out of it." In mentioning this factor, she sums up her need to be treated as an autonomous and competent adult; without such an attitude, assistance becomes merely a handout.

By contrast, we heard repeated stories about other homeless shelters that were noteworthy for their oppressive living conditions and apparently manipulative rules. Two religious facilities were singled out by many of our respondents for condemnation. Examples of serious health problems were cited, including overcrowding, terrible food, and epidemics. Residents accuse these shelters of taking most of their homeless assistance money for rent and not returning it to them when they leave. Some of these shelters required attendance at religious services, a demand that offended many of the homeless adults. One person seemed to speak for others who had stayed in those shelters when she said, "They berate you. They try to reduce you to as meaningless a mass as possible, mentally and physically, to which you're not able to do better. Then they can manipulate you."

The shelter agenda is often unstated, except in very general terms. But residents pick up quite easily on symbols, sent in subtle ways by both staff and the physical layout itself. When comparing shelters, some of their differences speak volumes about their priorities. For example, how much space is devoted to private counseling rooms? How much assistance is provided for job counseling or apartment hunting? How much responsibility are residents given for cooking and cleaning? The answers to such questions create an environment that either upholds or destroys the resident's sense of purpose and hope.

The locations of the shelters in Los Angeles County are another significant factor impinging on the dignity of the residents. Neither employment nor transportation are often located near shelter locations, making it that much more difficult for the homeless to find work or do the necessary apartment hunting to escape from their present situation. And because of a "not in my backyard" attitude, the tendency to ghettoize the homeless is simply one more factor removing them from the mainstream of society during the period of their most severe problems.

A somewhat sad example of the subjective nature of what constitutes a true shelter appears in a newspaper account about a New Mexico man who sold doghouses. Concerned about the homeless problem in his city, he added three feet to the length of his doghouses and installed windows and a door, then took them to a lot where homeless people were living. His well-meaning offer was not appreciated by the people, and "a city official told [him] that his doghouses for the homeless were 'dehumanizing, degrading and disgusting.' " Someone even urinated on one of them in protest. He tried again with a larger design but was then informed that it looked more like an outhouse than a shelter. Frustrated, he moved to another city, where he finally found a small group of people who preferred his converted doghouses to sleeping outside.[7]

Similar problems arise in the response of city residents and public officials to the more informal forms of shelter utilized by homeless people who cannot (or choose not to) live in more acceptable shelters. For example, in 1987 the city of Los Angeles began a series of crackdowns on Skid Row homeless encampments, including raids by police officers and sanitation and social workers. After a series of confrontations, the people were allowed to sleep anywhere along the street as long as they did not build any "makeshift quarters" and as long as they were not in front of businesses, even at night. While the business community applauded the moves, homeless activists criticized the policy for undermining the one mode of survival left to this group of people. The policy was finally reversed, although the tensions were not resolved.[8]

Clearly the more fundamental issue raised by such examples is, What constitutes an acceptable shelter, and what is destroyed or threatened when individuals and families no longer have a more usual form of housing? We can convert doghouses or allow people to sleep on the streets in front of stores or provide cardboard boxes and open heating grates. But such responses merely underscore the fact that what is missing is a home, a stable and safe environment providing the essentials of dignity for people in trouble.

Shelter Rules

No issue is mentioned as often as shelter rules. Even when people realize the need for such rules, they usually complain how they feel constrained, undermined, and limited by them. Nothing threatens the autonomy of homeless families as much as the imposition of stringent shelter rules over which they have no influence as conditions for their continued residence in the shelter.

Shelters vary enormously in terms of rules and services provided. Most shelters require some counseling, and family shelters are much more likely to do so than other facilities. Regulations vary widely, although most shelters prohibit alcohol or drug use and insist on certain health and conduct requirements. A wide range of policies have developed regarding length of stay, with most shelters housing people for one or two months.[9]

Curfews are particularly important symbols of the infantilization of homeless adults. However necessary such limits may be, their effect is to remind people that their time is not their own, that they are being treated the way they treat their own children. For example, having to eat institutional meals at set hours provides a reminder that you cannot attend to your own most basic needs. Some shelters prohibit televisions or smoking in the rooms, and many do not allow residents to place locks on their doors. Pets are usually not allowed. Parents often have to accompany their children whenever they leave their rooms. Most shelters expect residents to leave the facility for a few hours during the day. Residents often resent having to answer a battery of questions to enter the facility, feeling either that their privacy is being invaded or that they are required to lie about their past in order to find a place for their children to stay.

One woman summed up her ambivalent attitude by saying: "I like it here, and I appreciate them trying to help me, but it's just too much. . . . they make you feel like we're in prison." Another woman used almost identical language: "These people here are nice . . . and I'm very grateful for them helping me, but then again I feel like I'm in a jail without the bars. It's so restrictive. . . . We are trying to make this like our home. . . . Make it more comfortable, a more comfortable living environment."

Residents have little or no influence over the rules; they find them firmly established, usually posted on walls or doors throughout the facility. Some shelters provide informal opportunities for residents to meet and discuss policies, but the rules are not decided upon by the residents. To the extent that rules are perceived as a threat to the dignity appropriate for an adult, the lack of control over them is significant.

Similarly, the justifications for the rules are likely to undermine the residents' sense of trust and responsibility. Even in the shelters known for their attempts to skim the homeless population for the best and most reliable people, the rules are upheld by a shared appreciation that, without them, possessions and persons would be less secure. The usually unspoken assumption behind the rules is that people cannot be trusted to respect others. In addition, some rules are justified by a rationale that may be even more debilitating to a sense of dignity: namely, that many of these people are unable to do what is best for themselves. Forcing residents to leave the shelter during the day is often explained by the belief that without such a rule residents would simply stay in their rooms and waste their weeks in the shelter. Such a perception may indeed be true in many cases, but its truth does not alter the message that such a policy conveys.

A 1988 Institute of Medicine study points out the ways in which shelter rules often prevent people from escaping from their current situation. For example, forcing people to leave during the day or limiting the number of nights a person can remain plays a major role in the ways in which the homeless experience becomes a vicious cycle.

> For chronically homeless people, however, such policies not only limit their ability to develop relatively more stable patterns of activities of daily living (e.g., developing a personal grooming routine, maintaining the cleanliness of their clothes) but also impede their ability to find employment as a way out of homelessness (homeless people cannot inform a prospective employer where they can be contacted if they do not know where they are going to be).[10]

But rules can be important mechanisms for defending the rights and status of the residents of homeless shelters. Because shelters are privately run in Los Angeles County, there are enormous differences in the ways in which they are structured and maintained, and the problem of standardizing rules and procedures in the shelters is an extremely complicated one. In Los Angeles an extensive effort occurred several years ago to develop a set of minimum standards that all homeless shelters would agree upon. The plan faltered due to the refusal of several facilities to agree to the specific rules. But the effort pointed out the concern of many homeless advocates that some such minimum standards are necessary for the protection of the residents. One interesting question is whether more systematic guidelines for all shelters are needed, or whether diversity is a positive development, allowing people to find (or be found by) the shelters that meet their particular needs at the moment.

It is interesting, for our purposes, to note that the proposed draft of standards for the shelters included as essential the provision of "humane care which preserves individual dignity." Among the other rights listed as essential were religious liberty, presenting grievances without fear of reprisal, confidentiality, freedom from restraint or confinement, receiving visitors "in designated areas during reasonable hours," and leaving and returning "at reasonable hours in accordance with the rules of the shelter."[11]

As a response to the lack of standardization, a set of informal policies was developed to deal with certain facilities. For example, one of the major referral agencies in Los Angeles refused to refer people to any shelter where at least two legitimate and outrageous complaints had been reported. (At the time of our study, approximately ten to twenty shelters had been placed on this list at least once.)

Concern over the nature of shelter rules raises some difficult issues, and no overall solution is apparent. It may be more important to bear in mind the extent to which rules of all sorts—whether dealing with curfews, financial independence, or control over one's children—represent society's ultimate assessment of the residents during their stay in the shelter. Whatever style of life, personal rights, or opportunities may formally exist outside, the residents' only universe of moral and legal sanctioning becomes the four walls of the shelter, and the only human sign of how society responds is embodied in the shelter workers.

As we would expect, the same value conflicts that shape all of us continue to affect the ways in which shelter residents are viewed and treated. We cannot be surprised to find paternalism mixed with prodding, praise mixed with blame, assertiveness mixed with hopelessness; shelter workers can only reflect to the residents the wider society's difficulties in identifying with and responding to their situation.

Social Services and the Shelters

Should shelters provide more services for their residents? Most shelters provide very few, and shelter residents often complain about their need for more job training, personal counseling, assistance in seeking a permanent place to live, and child care.[12] One observer commented astutely that the main function of the shelter system is not to house people but rather to funnel information and benefits to them, largely because the welfare system is more comfortable dealing with providers than with homeless people themselves. Indeed, shelters may be crucial entry points into the social service system.

These observations say more about the way the broader system functions than they do about the shelters themselves. Because of lack of information, inefficiency, ignorant or hostile workers, and the complexity of negotiating the system, many homeless people (as is the case for poor people in general) are not receiving all of their benefits. Shelters usually provide staff who can intervene and pressure the system to respond more adequately.

But various advocates have pointed out that such services should in fact be provided by the society at large rather than by each separate facility. Most of the services needed by the homeless are also needed by poor people in general. Indeed, the cost of decentralizing these services into each shelter may be more expensive than simply paying people to move into an apartment of their own.

A related question concerns the outstationing of welfare system offices in the shelters themselves. We heard very mixed responses to this policy of sending social service workers to shelters on a regular basis, thus freeing the residents from having to spend time and effort going to welfare offices. While the advantages are generally recognized, some shelter workers were concerned about being too closely identified with the system itself; they tend to see their roles at the moment as advocates for their residents, helping them deal with the system and obtaining the benefits to which they are entitled. The underlying issue is the role the shelters will play in helping homeless families.

Shelters and the Homeless Problem

Are shelters part of the problem or part of the solution? If we expect these facilities to solve the complex interconnected family and social problems responsible for the homelessness of hundreds of thousands of our fellow citizens, then we will be disappointed and discouraged. On the other hand, as places where people can be temporarily housed and fed and receive a brief period of respite within which to try to regroup and redirect their energies, shelters play an important and unfortunately indispensable role in the current situation.

In terms of our concern about dignity, we have identified a number of ways in which the shelter system makes it difficult for people to maintain or rekindle their sense of self-esteem and self-respect. In spite of the best intentions and available resources on the part of the providers, it should not surprise us that many people have a negative and defensive view of these opportunities.

Consider the example of a woman who demonstrates how insisting on a sense of dignity can make it difficult to receive help from shelters at all. She was referred first to a shelter that she says "is not a good place for nobody, because the lady took all the information from you and everything." Having been repelled by the personal intrusion and demands, she was referred to another shelter where she would have had to sleep on the floor. "I told her, 'Well, thank you anyway, but I'm not going to sleep on the floor, me and my two kids, because I don't know how clean that floor is.' " Saying the staff woman had "a little attitude," the woman decided to sleep in her car, saying that "I'm not sleeping on nobody's floor, no matter what."

What are our reactions to this account? Is she an ungrateful person who is not willing to accept an offer of help? Or is she someone with a strong enough sense of her own dignity to refuse to be treated in certain ways by anyone, even someone offering help?

The more we listen to the experiences of these families, the more we recognize the many little ways in which shelter life continually undermines independence and self-esteem. For example, when phones are placed in public places, people cannot have a private phone conversation with a friend, relative, or potential employer. It is not sufficient to allude to the need for surveillance or the financial dangers of allowing people to make long-distance phone calls; the effect on people's lives is to undermine any sense of the privacy and autonomy that is essential to enable them to take the steps necessary to move on with their (and their families') lives.

Shelters are at their best in providing residents some measure of safety and security and also some valuable short-term predictability. In this way they are able to provide a context for recreating a sense of dignity about one's life, allowing people time to reflect and begin making plans concerning their future. Although it would strike most of us as a frighteningly short time, two months of respite can appear like a lifetime to someone who has been living from night to night in cheap hotels. Parents can think about enrolling children in school, looking for a job and an apartment, and moving on.

But the predictability can be misleading, particularly for people who have significant problems taking control of their lives. Day follows day, week follows week—and they find themselves at the end of their stay with some money saved up but little prospect for a stable future. Several people we interviewed were near the end of their time in the shelter, and most of them were still looking for both work and apartments. Unless major changes occur during their shelter stay, people's lives are unlikely to be very different when they leave. It is not the fault of the shelters, for the task of remaking a life cannot be accomplished in a few weeks. But it is a depressing reality of the shelter system that so few opportunities exist for people to use this time to turn a life of chaos and confusion into a more stable and predictable future.

Finally, it is worth noting that one response to the inadequacy of assistance has been the development of a homeless advocacy movement in American cities. In Los Angeles, for example, a wide range of organizations serve the homeless population, and some fairly bitter disputes have developed concerning their agendas and ideologies. One of the continuing conflicts stems from the tension between accepting and needing governmental assistance and the fear of governmental control and guidance. For example, the Los Angeles

County Coalition on the Homeless was created in the mid-1980s. It was primarily county-funded and conservative. By 1990, however, the group had been taken over by more liberal advocacy groups, which changed the name to the Coalition *for* the Homeless, and it receives no government money.

But tension exists between the advocates and the homeless. To what extent should advocates (most of whom are likely to be middle-class and white) speak for the homeless? Although some indigenous movements are beginning to arise among the homeless themselves, their organizational problems are enormous due to the instability of the population. We would expect that so long as shelters provide such an important temporary haven for homeless people, they will continue to operate—and so will conflict between providers and the homeless themselves. From the standpoint of the staff and financial backers, too many elements of shelter life make it impossible or inadvisable to give the residents more control. As long as this is the case, many shelters will inevitably undermine the dignity of their residents despite providing a much-needed haven for people to gain some breathing space in the midst of their very troubled lives.

PART THREE

Making Sense of Homelessness

5

Coping with Being Homeless

The dignity that homeless persons experience depends in part on how others treat them—on whether they are humiliated by the welfare system and whether the staff in the shelter where they are living treats them with respect. But dignity is also something that people struggle with on a purely personal level. Dignity is a matter of self-interpretation, and hence homeless people are in need of protective armor to shield their self-respect.

We can protect our dignity in many ways in threatening situations, and all of these ways are familiar even to those of us who have been spared such harsh crises in our own lives. We can rationalize our circumstances, deny what is happening to us, or stubbornly hope that things will get better. We can resign ourselves to what is happening or adopt a reduced set of expectations or a diminished self-image in order to deal with brutal realities in our lives. In particular, however, when human beings find themselves in difficult situations from which they cannot physically escape, they often attempt to escape psychologically. This takes the form of distancing themselves from both the situation and from other persons who share their current crisis.

In this chapter we will focus on distancing mechanisms as one key example of how homeless people cope with their situations. No value judgment is implied in recognizing that people distance themselves from their life situations. Such defense mechanisms are perfectly normal, particularly when escape by other means is either impossible or too costly for other reasons. Monica Scott's story illustrates the variety of mechanisms used and the difficulties that several of them pose as she attempts to maintain dignity in the face of her homelessness.

Monica Scott

Monica Scott is living in a shelter with her three young children, ranging in age from three to six years old. She is a divorced twenty-two-year-old white woman who is having housing problems for the first time in her life. Her parents divorced when she was young, but her mother remarried a man with a good job and they bought a nice home in Montana. Ms. Scott became pregnant when she was fifteen years old and ended up in a physically abusive marriage with an alcohol- and drug-addicted husband. She finally left him after some severe beatings, and she eventually had to leave the area because he kept finding her and beating her up.

She arrived in Los Angeles (where her mother had just moved) with her three children, just a month before we interviewed her in the shelter. She stayed with her mother for a couple of days but had to leave because her mother's apartment complex does not allow children. She went to the Travelers' Aid Society, which finally found a space for her in the shelter.

Her response to what has happened to her is revealed in the way she speaks about her present situation. Her main effort is to convince us that she is not a typical poor person who is used to being homeless or on welfare. For example, she begins by reporting that the worker at Travelers' Aid said to her, "When I saw you come in, I saw me several years ago, and I could see you were someone who really wanted, who was a worker." She insists, "I'm not a lazy butt," and, in a fascinating metaphor for her own life and appearance, she tells us proudly that she wishes that "someone could see me, because my car is a '78, it's a cute car on the inside but on the outside there's rust on it, and I get comfortable because I see people see my car."

She distinguishes herself carefully from other people who are living with her in the shelter. She tells us sadly that "it seems like everyone here in the homeless shelter has done drugs except for me. Everybody says they smoke weed and stuff, and that's not the reason I'm homeless." Saying that people should be screened for such activities, she suggests that the welfare system should cut people off after two years unless there is a severe medical problem, and she backs up her position by recounting her own experiences in the welfare offices. "I saw the people sitting there, and the smell, and the dirt, and the lazy butts sitting there. . . . These people are going there and collecting it from my taxes. I work hard. I work hard for things! And here these people are sitting there expecting the state to pay them."

Her anger is apparent as she compares the attitude of another woman to her own. "I saw a welfare woman in Montana, the one whose kiddies pee onto my porch and stuff. And she goes, 'Well, if the state of Montana could guarantee me that my kids' fathers will pay child support, I'd get off of welfare.' Well, who in the hell is the state of Montana to guarantee that your kids, those aren't the state of Montana's kids. Those are yours! You work for them!" She even suggests tying the tubes of women on welfare who have too many children and throwing single men off of the welfare rolls completely. She concludes her comments by saying, "I'm getting tired of supporting people who don't want to support themselves."

We would hear the same theme throughout the course of her conversations with us. She is careful to tell us that she has never had housing problems before, that she has always had custody of her children, and that "I get depressed when the state's supporting me, and it's like I feel like I'm just a typical welfare mom, and . . . it makes me depressed because *I* can't even support me and my children." She insists that "I don't like going for handouts. I'm very independent. I've never ever just quit a job to go get on welfare. I love to work, because I feel, I already know that I can, I work well with people."

She is committed to viewing herself as someone who simply does not fit in with either the lifestyle or the environment of other homeless people. "I've never lived in a ghetto, this is awful. . . . In Montana, we don't have the gangs, and we don't have people sitting on the sidewalk shooting up." She says, "I come from clean standards, cleaner living." She is so out of place that she can hardly communicate with these people: "I guess a lot of the people here have been drug abusers, because you listen to them talk and I don't understand what they're saying."

When she imagines what her life will be like in the future, she sees radical changes, including owning a beautiful home, taking in foster children, and owning her own company. She wants to be in a situation "where I will look back on this and think it was all a bad dream. And everyone else, if they ever thought of that, they'd laugh, thinking if I was ever in something like that, no one would believe it."

It is the present that is odd, unusual, and unrepresentative of the true state of affairs. Believing this can make it much easier to look in the mirror of her life and continue to affirm that she is, like the pilgrim always on the move, "in but not of" this present madness and confusion. The sense of unreality Ms. Scott feels about the present is revealed in her insistence that, someday, other people will view her as someone who could never have been homeless.

As we examine a variety of forms of distancing, many of Ms. Scott's types of responses and reasoning will reappear. However odd or even inappropriate some of her interpretations might appear to be, they must be understood as important and perhaps healthy ways of defending her sense of dignity and identity from the onslaughts of a life that has turned out so very differently from what she always imagined.

In the next section we turn to a variety of ways in which homeless people attempt to distance themselves in order to make sense of, and live with, the fact that they are without permanent shelter.

Denial as a Means of Distancing

Although denial is, properly understood, a separate form of psychic protection, it can be seen as one end of a spectrum of distancing responses. What better way is there to put distance between the self and its present painful condition than to deny that the condition exists at all?

Of course, people can hardly deny that they are living in a shelter or on the streets or that they are dependent on welfare to feed their children. But it is quite possible to refuse to deal with the situation, to either ignore it or deny its significance entirely. Whether someone can continue to do so for an extended period of time, or without serious threats to other elements of personal well-being, is another question.

Asked how she was handling her present situation, a woman responded by saying: "I don't really know, I don't even think about it really. I just say, some way, somehow, we're going to get—we're not going to sleep in the streets, we know that, that's how I feel." When we asked whether she was anxious or depressed, she said: "I don't really think about my problems, I don't really think about them at all. I don't really feel nothing sometimes." She is denying not so much the fact that she is homeless as the fact that this situation is affecting her in ways that she must think and feel about. All of us have experienced situations that were simply too painful to think about and have engaged in some form of psychic numbing as a response.

A more graphic example of denial is found in the story told by a woman whose husband left her several months ago to move in with another woman. In spite of extensive evidence to the contrary, this respondent continues to insist that her husband still loves her, that he will soon return to her, and that the other woman "can't fill my shoes." When asked what her worst experience has been, she is unable to admit that her situation has been hard for her compared to earlier periods when she "had a couple of nervous breakdowns." She says: "I just have a strong mind, so it's hard for me to, my mind, even being hit or pushed, I don't feel the pain. I've had bruises, I don't feel it."

It would be hard to think of a clearer example of denial functioning as a form of distancing the self from a painful set of experiences. We can understand why it would be so threatening for this woman to admit that her husband may have left her because he was more in love with someone else and to recognize that she is in fact incapable at the moment of providing for herself and her family. We do not need to judge her in order to recognize that she simply cannot accept the implications of what has been happening to her.

The paradox here, at least from the perspective of the observer, is that denial, while acknowledging the pain that threatens the self-image of an autonomous person, may pose an even more serious threat to that person's dignity in the long run. People who are deeply in denial are likely to continue making very significant mistakes in judging which parts of the world are really under their control and what is likely to happen next. For this woman to continue to expect her husband to return to her, however understandable this wish might be, is to deprive herself of the ability to make decisions that might lead to different consequences. As a result, the longer she remains in denial, the longer she remains a victim.[1]

Minimizing the Situation

Just short of denial, we find people struggling to minimize their situations. They recognize that something is wrong but adopt an "it isn't so bad" attitude. This perspective allows them to believe that they are not in particularly bad shape, and thereby they diminish the gap between how they view themselves and the reality of the situation they find themselves in.

For example, a woman residing in a shelter bristles at the very term "homeless," even though she admits to having stayed outside occasionally: "I haven't had to be homeless, really. It's just been overnight in a hotel, or whatever, camping out in a campsite or something. . . . But you know, you work it out." The act of redefinition is crucial; if I am not "really" homeless, then I am better off than those people who are.

We find a similar response from a woman who is optimistic about finding a job and moving into her own apartment. In speaking about her situation, she attempts to focus on the benefits of being homeless and compares herself to those who are much worse off than her: "It's also been kind of a very humbling thing when you want to think about it, because I know that there are people living here who are much worse off than I am. They are in much greater need than I am." She insists that although she is materially better able to deal with her life than most people around her, emotionally she remains deprived: "I think that basically I'm here because emotionally I needed it, very much. I did not have the resources at the time either, but still a lot of them come here and they don't even have any food or anything, and I do at least have my stuff in storage."

There is something admirable about this kind of response to being homeless. Comparing oneself to those who have even less can be both sustaining and humanizing, particularly if it leads to steps to improve both oneself and those who are worse off. But the danger of stepping over the line into a Pollyannaish viewpoint must not be overlooked. As observers, we are likely to be skeptical of a person in apparently obvious need who says that nothing is seriously wrong. To the extent that recognition of a problem is the first step in seeking to change, minimizing one's condition, like denial, can make it worse.

It should be clear that both denying and minimizing reality can undercut a person's ability to live out a responsible and ordered life. However protective and soothing such mechanisms may be, they are likely to be ineffective in making the problems disappear. Indeed, it is more likely that they will become ways to escape from confronting the hard choices and work that are usually required to turn one's life around.

Precisely because dignity is tied so closely to our ability to make decisions, to take control, and to lead predictable lives, these defense mechanisms are further steps in undermining an already fragile sense of worth and meaning. People are unlikely to take a homeless woman seriously or to view her as a stable and responsible adult if they perceive that she is unable or unwilling to face problems. Even more significant, she is unlikely to be able to view herself with a sense of dignity and self-respect as long as she cannot face what is happening to her.

Isolating the Present

A somewhat more sophisticated approach is similar to minimizing but is better able to accept the situation for what it is, in all its seriousness and discomfort. This response involves isolating the present as a distinct and clearly heterogeneous part of the flow of one's life; although the situation is bad now, it is only temporary, and things will "get back to normal" very soon.

We especially saw this sort of response when parents discussed how they tried to explain the situation to their children. A father says that his children are dealing fairly well with being homeless. He attributes their stability in part to his attempts to assure them that things will change for the better very soon. He reports that he keeps telling them, "Understand, we're here for right now, it's not going to be forever, we're going to move, don't worry your mom about 'I don't like it here, I don't want to be there,' because it will only make things worse."

A woman whose parents were alcoholics recalls the experiences of her childhood and is determined that her own children will not have to undergo such a traumatic and seemingly endless pattern of abuse and neglect: "That's why now, I tell my kids, I'll drink a beer now and then, but not like the kids I know, I've lived that life, there's no way I would give that life to my kids. . . . I tell them, 'We won't be here forever, we just have to make the best of it for now,' and they're very understanding, because they know I'm there, and everything I get is for them."

But these adults are also telling us, and themselves, that their situation is not permanent. The comments of homeless individuals often reveal a deep insistence that their present condition does not, and will not, define or confine them in the future. As observers of their lives, however, we might react by praising them for their optimism while wondering if there isn't an element of self-deception involved here. The ability to view the present as an aberration can lead to the inability to see broader patterns and, therefore, to taking more radical steps to change.

Class Distancing

One of the most frequent forms of distancing behavior is for people to claim that they are not really the sort of people who are typically homeless. We saw this response in Monica Scott's comments at the beginning of this chapter. Over one-quarter of the respondents were quite eager to point out that they had never before been homeless, or even poor, and that their family backgrounds were comfortable and reliable.

The best illustration of this sort of response is to quote a few interviewees:

> Just being out in the streets. I've never experienced that. I come from a fairly good home, a very good home. . . . I didn't even know about anything like that to tell you the truth, I was really sheltered. I didn't even know what a cockroach was until I was about seventeen, I had never seen one before.

> These were people who were like street people for years. . . . Sometimes it's different, because sometimes some people choose to live that way, or some people have been doing this for years, have been living on the street, and they know, they're streetwise. . . . I just kept feeling this overwhelming feeling of guilt and hurt, because my dad had so many kids and this had never happened to us, never! . . . This has been a very devastating experience for me.

> I never thought life would be like this, struggling and everything.

There are several intertwined messages contained in these statements. These comments show an obvious effort to report one's background. But beyond that, they reflect a need to separate oneself from incorrect conclusions people may draw from the fact of one's homelessness: namely, that you are one of the chronically homeless, part of the underclass of American society. In indicating that they are in fact not from that background, the interviewees distance themselves from the class situation of those who are.

The implications of these sorts of statements are made even more obvious by the mention of characteristics that are highly associated with class identity. For example, education is sometimes mentioned as setting the person apart. One woman believes she has received better treatment from society at large because of her class background: "I went to the right schools, and I got the best education. I lived in the Boston area, so it's a little bit easier for me."

Another woman sighs deeply when asked about her worst experience since becoming homeless, and she relates what has happened to her earlier (and more central) identity. She remembers that "for seven and a half years, all I did was work every day and go to school at night and study like crazy on the weekends." Now, however, she is frustrated to "find myself in this position." Although she recognizes that "at least my education can't go away from me," she still acknowledges that "it's just very hard coming to grips with the fact, I've done all this to get to a certain point, and now I'm in this position, and it's very frightening." Receiving a good education is supposed to provide a buffer from such situations; when it does not, you can still hold onto the fact that you remain well educated. In viewing yourself as well educated, you create a barrier between yourself and the usual image of the homeless person.

For other people, it is the fact that they have held regular jobs that reminds them (and should convince us) that they are not typical homeless people. Remember the earlier comment from the woman collecting AFDC benefits who insists that she is now drawing upon the money she paid in taxes when she worked for twenty years: "I feel as though I have just put money in the bank, and right now I'm drawing interest off of it. I'm just drawing interest off for a moment, just for a moment, because I do not intend to be an AFDC recipient the rest of my life." Instead of defining herself as a person dependent on the system, she claims she is merely receiving back what she was owed by virtue of her truer identity as a productive member of society.

Intelligence is another personal attribute that people use to disassociate themselves from stereotypes about the homeless. One woman speaks at length about her ability to speed-read, saying that she reads so quickly that she can't enjoy it. She claims that she has taught herself to read upside down in order to read more slowly, a procedure that creates odd stares when she is reading on a bus or in other public places. Another woman brags that she has an I.Q. of 148, "so how could I be a bimbo?"

Still other people focus on an entire set of lifestyle and personal value orientations that distance them, by virtue of background, from other home-less people. Asserting that people are formed primarily in their childhood experiences, one woman says: "My mother and my aunts and uncles, as far as cleanness, they demand cleanness. . . . I'm finding in California, you have more people that are unhealthy, . . . I really hate filth and nastiness." The meaning of asserting such a clear-cut difference between one's class position and that of the homeless is heard in the following comment by this same woman: "My father never wanted to see us on welfare, and I used to wonder why. . . . A lot of people *can* live off of it and be content, but I'm one of the type of person that I can't be content with, because I want more. I really hope and pray that I get the shot [at it]." As long as I continue to believe that this is not where I belong, I can believe that I can, and should be, somewhere else.

It might even be suggested that such self-definition is one of the most important features of any class system. To believe that they are really "the sort of people" who are lower- or middle- or upper-class, with all the attendant opportunities and powers associated with that class, provides people with a set of aspirations and definitions of what they can be expected to achieve. Conversely, such self-perceptions can limit us in our view of what we can achieve or acquire. Anyone who believes that there is no class system in American society has probably never listened to poor people speak about their prospects for advancement.

A key feature of many of these illustrative explanations is the claim that the person is somehow disoriented in the present situation, as though placed in an alien culture. Indeed, that is precisely the image people may wish to convey in order to suggest that they are from a different social world or class than that of the homeless and destitute.

For example, a woman details the murders and abuse she has witnessed while homeless and says that she has no idea how to begin to deal with such unique events, since "this is the first time in my life that I was able to see people getting murdered." Another woman complains about the sights on Skid Row and says that her children cannot stay in such a place: "My kids were seeing things, I was seeing things that I never known was true, you see on T.V., you never know things like that happen." The following account indicates how radically different the speaker's experiences are from her usual life experience:

> It was about four o'clock in the morning, it was freezing cold, I didn't have no coat for Allison, no coat for myself, no coat for my husband, and they made us go outside, and I mean, that was the scariest, these were people who were like street people for years. . . . Sometimes it's different, because sometimes some people choose to live that way, or some people have been doing this for years, have been living on the street, and they know, they're streetwise. We've always had a home. . . . People would give us the wrong directions purposely, even social workers giving us the wrong directions, because they knew we didn't know the town.

We find an interesting approach among the few interviewees who have been dependent on welfare for a long time. For them, the key step is to distance themselves in terms of their present orientation, using their past experiences to intensify their self-understanding as people who are no longer willing to live dependently. A woman tells the story of her childhood, when her parents were forced to live on welfare. She recounts the embarrassment of having social service workers make surprise visits to the house at eleven o'clock at night to see if all of the children were still living at home. Her present attitude is clearly shaped by these experiences:

> I remember all of that as a child, and I was determined that, no matter what, I would never do that when I was an adult, I would never live on welfare. So far I haven't, we've been on it one time, and that was for a month, and that was just to get medical coverage when I was pregnant with my son. We got the welfare, and

we got the medical coverage, and the day my son was born, my husband got a job and he's worked ever since, and other than the disability thing, we've never had to go—welfare is fine because there are a lot of people who could not make it, they have no other way, but I would rather do anything else than that.

Once again, we see the clear efforts at class distancing. Welfare is "fine" for other people "who could not make it, they have no other way," but she is the sort of person who would "rather do anything else than that," precisely because she has climbed *out* of the class situation where she must be dependent upon the system.

Scapegoating the Homeless

When carried to an extreme, distancing turns into a form of criticism, of blaming and judging other people for their condition. We are interested here in how and why some of the homeless themselves engage in the business of blaming the victim.

The milder form of such criticism is heard when people insist that they have tried hard to improve their own situations and suggest how unusual this is. For example, remember Ms. Scott's way of speaking about her desire to be independent: "I don't like going for handouts. I'm very independent. I've never ever just quit a job to go get on welfare." She is implying here that poor people do such things, while she obviously does not.

Similarly, turning the question of homelessness into one of willpower is a common way to distinguish oneself from others who refuse to make the effort to change their situations. One person says that the key is to "look at yourself honestly and see what caused you to become homeless" and then to act on this self-knowledge. "It has to come from within. There's going to have to come a time in your life that you got to get tired of being sick and tired of that. . . . then you're going to have to start making a conscious decision in yourself, in your heart, that you want to change the situation that you're in." This is an extremely common pattern of thought, usually accompanied by specific criticisms of people who either do not make the effort to improve or who are simply the type of people who are not interested in change.

The extent to which these comments resemble much of the rhetoric and assumptions of the Reagan era about America's poor is striking and somewhat distressing. For example, one of our respondents notes: "We've hit bottom, but we'll bounce back. You're not always going to stay at the bottom, unless you want to be that way." Similarly, a man is upset because "a lot of people just damn well don't want to work," and he complains that "there's a lot of single mothers here that just don't give a fuck, they're getting welfare and it doesn't matter."

We hear similar sentiments from a surprising number of other voices, a few of which we will quote briefly:

> I know there's nothing wrong with a lot of these homeless people. They're not disabled, they can read, they can write. It's not hard for them to maybe go out and find a job somewhere. It's hard, that's something that's reality, it's hard, you have to crawl before you walk.

> I believe that there are people that live off of welfare. . . . A lot of people that live off of welfare when they could work, and don't want to provide better for their family, and a lot of times they continue a cycle of their children become welfare children. Well, I don't hope to bring on that cycle, because I've taught my kids that, if I was able to work, I would be working!

> You wonder how people do it when they've got jewelry on and their nails are these acrylic nails, cost forty bucks. There's something wrong here, why are they collecting the welfare? Or girls that come from affluent families who end up with their families helping them and they're *still* collecting the welfare, and nothing happens. And I feel like I'm hanging myself out to dry every time I don't report everything quite clearly enough, because I know I could handle it and get this done.

One woman expresses disdain for people who go from shelter to shelter over a period of months or years, a pattern she interprets as meaning that they have no desire to improve their situation. She notes that some residents spend all of their time in their rooms and need to be kicked out of the shelter completely: "You can't pamper them. You can give them an inch, they expect a mile. We've got a couple who came in . . . who aren't grateful at all, they're living in the place free."

Shelter residents also often draw a sharp distinction between their peers on the basis of the use of drugs and alcohol. A common assumption among the people we interviewed is that drug abuse involves either laziness or a lack of will and that people who are alcoholics or drug abusers belong to the category of the undeserving poor. What is most interesting is the sharpness of the distinction, the assumption that certain people become addicts and others (namely, the speakers) do not.

This tendency is revealed, for example, in one woman's insistence that she has not engaged in drug dealing or prostitution: "I wouldn't even go that way. I don't care how bad problems get, I wouldn't do that." Again, it is purely her character, rather than her situation, that explains why she abstains from certain sorts of behavior. Another person speaks angrily about drug users, suggesting that the problem could easily be solved by simply rounding them up and placing them in a desert prison for ten years.

One obvious reason for this distancing by the interviewees is fear that they will be lumped in with such people. Many people even comment that there are sufficient shelter services for people like them, but that something needs to be done about drug addicts and alcoholics, making sure that they are not allowed to stay in the same shelters. For example, listen to the following description of drug abusers:

> Now those that lay in the street, maybe they want to be out there in the street. . . . Some people . . . drug addicts, a drug addict . . . wants to get money, whatever, they go get their drugs, then they get out on the street again. . . . If you don't help yourself, who's going to help you? . . . One thing they need to do . . . homeless people that are on drugs, they need to be in a different shelter. . . . People that are not on drugs and having problems about paying rent and low income, that should be a different spot. . . . So I think that's one of the things that they need to do. . . . They will make it bad for other people.

Similar comments are made by a woman concerned about such people staying in their shelters: "In a way it's sort of mean to say, but a lot of the people that are attracted to these type of places are people that are on drugs, and there are the people that really need to get in these places that don't have anything to do with drugs. . . . I think what they should do is maybe do some kind of drug test or something like that for the people that are coming into these type of shelters."

Some people adopt a somewhat more sympathetic tone, but the stereotype of addicts and alcoholics (however true it may be) remains—that these people are unable and unwilling to take care of themselves. In the following quotation, for example, the more compassionate tone is mingled with the familiar distancing: "I have the mind to [be able to support my kids], because I'm not a drug user, I'm not an alcoholic, so that freed me a whole lot. It's even more to the women who use it, because if they don't know a way out to get help for themselves as far as drugs, they're going to use the money they have to buy drugs, so they are more stuck, it's like they're more helpless."

Conclusion

Sometimes distancing works, and sometimes it fails. As one woman admits, there is a point at which you have to recognize that you are, in fact, homeless: "I used to see people going down to this building and standing out, and I used to always wonder, what is this, and now I know what it is, because I'm here with them."

The motives for adopting various sorts of distancing language and claims are complex, but the central point is that homelessness threatens the personal dignity of those it traps. Perhaps if homeless people were more convinced that their underlying sense of worth would be upheld regardless of their living conditions or financial situation, they would be much less likely to adopt the various strategies we have outlined in this chapter.

Once again, the range of responses reminds us of our own attempts to distance ourselves from homeless people. We suspect that the reader can identify with most of these psychological maneuvers and recognize that they serve as effective ways to avoid either confronting homeless people or responding to them. Who among us has not felt that "this could never happen to me," or "I was raised to avoid such situations," or "my problems are only temporary and don't reflect who I really am"? The need to maintain a sense of dignity is no less deep among people who have been stripped of the visible signs of social status, and their efforts at distancing differ from ours primarily in that they seem more apparent.

It is particularly saddening to recognize the extent to which homeless people accept the broader society's stereotypes of their motives and character. By going to such lengths to distance themselves from other homeless people, they tacitly accept these stereotypes, implying that they are true for others but not for them. Indeed, this may be one of the greatest and most debilitating effects of homelessness: in a society that does not reaffirm the basic dignity of each person, the loss of a home becomes a terrifying status that must be denied or reinterpreted at all costs, even at the price of undercutting solidarity with other people in a similar position.

6

Finding Meaning in
Being Homeless

When we spoke with her, Barbara Kelly was a twenty-five-year-old black single pregnant woman living in the shelter with the youngest of her three children. She had been evicted from her last apartment when she was unable to pay the rent and had been bouncing around between shelters and friends' homes for the last couple of weeks.

Her childhood was difficult, but she says that "we never had to do without." Her mother was on welfare after divorcing her father; this did not seem like a major deprivation, however, since they lived in an area where "everybody was on welfare." She ran away from home when she was fourteen, believing that her family "just didn't care enough for me." She married a man who abused her, and she is pregnant now from another brief relationship. She has held a few cashier jobs at minimum wage, but she hasn't worked for a year because "I was just tired of doing it, it's not enough money for me and the baby."

She tells a story of years filled with "very terrible things"; being homeless, by comparison, is "really nothing for me." She was kidnapped and shot, and she was raped several times many years ago. She feels she has suffered from severe racial discrimination, particularly from Mexicans in neighborhoods where she has looked for places to live. And she is having a very difficult time in the shelter. She complains about the rules and the fact that the staff will not let her discipline her child the way she wants to: "You have to go by their rules when you're here, so that's why when I get my own apartment, it's going to be different, and my child is going to have to get used to it."

How does she deal with what has been happening? Throughout the interview she refers to ways in which God has helped her. What has kept her going is just having faith that God really will do something: "It's greater than whatever you can do, it's inside, the Lord knows your heart, he knows the inside of your soul. It's really great when you feel like that. It saved my life all these years. . . . Everybody needs different things." When she was most terrified about being out on the street with her young son, what saved her was the fact that "I just knowed that I had to really stop whining about it, put my faith in Jesus that he won't let us be on the street." All she hopes for is that Jesus will continue to act in and on her life, because "your life is already planned. . . . Jesus makes plans for you. . . . I don't make plans ahead, I just take it as it comes."

She attributes the fact that things are not even worse to divine intervention. She notes proudly that she never had to live on the street and that her mother took the family in during her last pregnancy. She seems convinced that in spite of all that has happened, "the Lord is always working miracles for me." Ms. Kelly also reveals a certain sense of hopelessness or apathy about what will happen in the future. She finds it very difficult to speculate about where she will be in five years, saying: "I don't see anything, I can't see that far. I might be dead five years from now." She says she hopes to get married eventually but laments, "I don't even have a boyfriend." She attributes her problems with men to the fact that "they can't deal with me because I'm a real person. . . . I don't even have friends, I don't have nobody, I'm just by myself."

Her religious interpretations are perhaps the only source of meaning and connection she can experience at this point in her life. Not only do they allow her to avoid drawing the conclusion that she is entirely on her own, they also provide comfort and reassurance that things will get better because someone else is really in charge. She is torn between her insistence on her own independence and strength (particularly in relation to her son's discipline and her living conditions) and her fear that nothing will ever change unless someone else (namely God) can intervene in her life.

The Need for a Higher Frame of Reference

Barbara Kelly's references to God represent a desire held by many individuals to understand life from a deeper frame of reference than social circumstances. Ms. Kelly believes that there is a divine plan at work in her life that makes sense out of otherwise meaningless events. There is more to her life than meets the eye. If not, then she would feel desperate, because the events taken in isolation present a very bleak picture of her prospects. Her sense of personal dignity and hope rests in her faith that Jesus is making plans for her.

Freud, Marx, and other critics of religion have viewed appeals to divine legitimation and explanation as an opiate or childlike escape from reality. This is one perspective, and certainly one that has a long tradition in the social sciences. But it is also possible to see transcendent hope as more than mere projection, even as a positive, rather than a negative, quest for meaning.

Indeed, when questions of meaning are no longer asked, then an essential component of our humanity has been lost. Someone who has given up looking for a larger interpretive framework of meaning has been dehumanized in an important way.

As finite, mortal beings, we are acutely aware of our limitations and of the myriad ways in which we are unable to control our environments, our lives, or even our feelings. But most of us also possess an awareness that we are more than finite, or at least that these limitations do not completely define or capture us. Something urges us to go beyond—to ask about where we come from and where we are going, to imagine ourselves connected to a realm beyond our everyday world. Whether we refer to this dimension in explicitly religious terms or not, the search for meaning confronts us with a set of questions that are not simply part of our secularized everyday lives.

In part, this spiritual dimension of meaning is connected with the fact that we can never be sure what something means. There is an inherently subjective and even arbitrary element in saying that an event *means* something. The spiritual dimension is not a realm of certainty but one of intuition. We ask for explanations and assurances but must settle for guesses and hunches. Yet we do not stop seeking for meaning, precisely because most people are unwilling (or unable) to simply accept what happens to them without asking difficult and unanswerable questions. The fact that people continue to ask about meaning in the midst of their worst experiences can even be interpreted as an important indication of how very important that need for dignity remains in all of us, and how hard it is to give up.

Because almost all of our homeless family members spoke in terms of some form of traditional religious belief, that will be the focus of our discussion of their search for meaning. Their attempts to understand how God is involved in their lives represent their best efforts to find meaning in what is happening to them and to continue to believe that their lives somehow make sense. Although the range of responses we discuss are quite varied, the need for meaning is shared by all the respondents. They exhibit an implicit or explicit faith that the unfolding events of their troubled lives do not deny or separate them from God.

Vague Religiosity

Belief in God can be maintained without a concomitant belief that God has much to do with specific life events. Such a position is often described in terms of a very private transcendent faith or prayer life that does not seem to impinge on one's external life.

One woman's response to our question about God's role is a good example: "Yeah, I believe in God. He didn't help me through a lot of things, but I don't get into all that other kind of religious stuff, all that cult stuff. I pray, I do my own praying." While religion functions as a supporting factor in her life, she shies away from making any explicit connection: "I used to say, 'Well, I'll do it on my own, and I don't need to pray,' all this and that, I have my own beliefs, and there are some things now, I still have God and I believe."

Another woman says that God is "doing what he can. . . . I don't think God has anything to do with what I'm going through on this, I don't know. But I believe in God. I don't think he's the one causing it." When asked specifically whether God has any part at all in the solution of her problems, she responds no.

For other people, the connection between faith in God and the current situation is either unreflective or confused. One person says: "I pray every night. I don't think there's any relation between my situation and God per se. I do believe that if I didn't have the faith that I do, I'd probably be a lot worse off." Another woman denies that there is a connection between God and her problems but then states that "everything has a purpose" and that God must have a plan for what is happening to her family.

Such comments may frustrate us until we can recognize how they tie into broader perceptions of religion in our culture. It should be remembered that most sectors of our society have a virtual prohibition against denying God's existence. Public opinion polls repeatedly reveal that well over 90 percent of Americans continue to profess belief in God, and the separation of religion and state does not prevent us from including references to God in almost all our national ceremonies and rituals.[1] It is as if we feel that at least some obeisance to God's existence, and to one's relationship with that God, is expected, even if nothing specific can be said about it.

The few antireligious comments by the respondents are surprising because they are so rare. They seem to come most frequently from people who were raised in strict religious families and who have moved away from any religious identification as adults. One woman raised as a Mormon says: "I can see how people can get so wrapped up in a religion in a situation like this, because they need somebody to believe in, when they don't believe in themselves. And it's like, I'm telling you, I believe in me, and I've had a hard time just sticking that out."

God as Judge

The Western religious traditions raise a set of problems about the existence of evil and suffering because of the nature of the deity their followers worship. What is commonly known as the problem of theodicy arises because of three claims, held together in tension: God is the all-powerful creator of everything that is, and he is an all-good loving and caring force; yet evil and suffering exist in the world this loving God created.

On a philosophical plane, we can seemingly solve the dilemma of why a good God would have created a world with such evil and suffering by denying, or at least reinterpreting, any one of these three claims. We can assert that God really is not the creator of everything or that God's power is limited. Or we can say that God does not care enough to create a different sort of world. Or we can try to deny the existence of the evil and suffering that seem to have created the dilemma in the first place.[2]

Our respondents functioned as amateur theologians as they sought to deal with the same problem—how to explain the existence of suffering. Most people seem to try to find some way to connect their religious faith with their present situation without denying the existence of either a good and powerful God or imperfection and pain in the world.

One possible answer is that suffering is deserved. Although few people adopted the view that God was punishing them for their sins, it surfaced often enough to bear examination. Women especially espoused this view.

It is not surprising that so many women reveal extremely poor self-images, and that they tend to blame themselves for everything that happened to them. We believe it is important to place statements about religious judgment in this broader context, for it is likely that the more fundamental tendency is to attribute everything negative that happens to one's own failings rather than to God. Perhaps the most compelling and sad example of such thinking can be found in the comments of a thirty-seven-year-old single mother who had recently escaped from an abusive marriage at the time of her interview. In recounting her experience with her partner's drug use and physical violence, she reveals her belief that she is at fault: "I couldn't figure out if it was me, I was saying, maybe I'm not cooking right, or maybe the house isn't clean enough, I was thinking it was me. . . . I'm trying to be Miss Perfect . . . but come to find out it wasn't me, it was him."

In another example, an older woman is convinced that she must have done something wrong to earn the suffering she has been undergoing: "I believe that God do nothing for a reason. I must have done something in my lifetime to be in this shape. He is punishing me for something that I have did. . . . He's not letting me down, he's showing me what I don't need to do and what I need to do, and when he does make up in his mind that he's going to help me, I'm going to come up." She recognizes that the major problem with this explanation is that her children are also suffering for her mistakes, and she does not fully understand why. But she insists that God doesn't mean to be punishing them—rather, "It's got to get through to me—I'm the one. Whatever I did, or whatever I'm doing, when I make up in my mind that it's wrong, then everything will be better."

A married couple adopts the same attitude. The wife says, "I don't blame God and I don't fault God, because I know if I was doing what I *should* be doing as a religious person, as a mother, as a wife, then I wouldn't be in this predicament, not like this." Her husband responds that he feels the same way and that "you're old enough to know right from wrong, and basically that's what it comes down to. God was right, and what was said was right, and I'm doing wrong, and I know it isn't right."

Sometimes the sense of judgment is very precise and stark. One woman has recently discovered a fundamentalist apocalyptic version of Christianity and is convinced that the world is caught up in a cycle of divine retribution. When asked whether her particular problems are also part of this plan, she replies: "Probably, we're all part of it. It's like God is just saying, 'Okay, I'm just waiting for you guys, come on, keep blowing things [laughs], I'll get you [laughs].' "

People may be caught in their own judgmental attitude, particularly when trying to make sense of their situation to their children. One woman, who was brought up in a strict religious family, says she is ashamed to go to church because of her present situation. Her young son is now beginning to lose his faith, doubting "that there could be a God when this happens." Her response to him is to insist that "He [God] didn't do it, I did it, it was me, I made the wrong decision. But now He's going to help us out of it." But her son refuses to go to church, and we can guess that the mother's explanation looks even more unconvincing to him than it might to an outside observer.

It is worth noting that a few people explicitly deny the interpretation that they are being punished or judged. For example, a woman who sees no effect of religion on her problems insists, "We don't believe that God sits up there and points his finger at somebody and says, this is going to happen to you. We don't believe that. So if things aren't going right, you don't get mad at God." And another woman thinks back to the extremely judgmental attitude of her mother-in-law: "She'd always say, 'You're going to go to hell for smoking.' I'd say, 'That's okay, you're going to go to hell with me for judging.' "

God as Protector

Another way that people can find meaning in what is happening to them is to believe that God protects them no matter what may happen. Thus their suffering is given meaning by reaffirming their faith.

One woman in a religiously mixed marriage describes herself as "a born-again Christian" and reports that she prays often and hard about her problems: "We believe God will help us find what we need and if we do our part and keep trying, things will work out." She believes that God is indeed answering her prayers: her serious health problems are in remission, and their arrival at the shelter has improved their prospects.

Another woman reports that she believes that God is "with me and helping me, and guiding me, because a lot of things that I had set out to do, I never would have come through if he hadn't been by my side." This understanding of God as guide is shared by another homeless woman who says: "I thank God for everything, every little thing, I'm thanking Jesus for everything, for the shelter, and even my children are saying, 'Thank you Jesus for everything.' And it's been a lot of help. And I know that God will open more doors for me and my family." Note the ways in which such an attitude allows her to have faith in the future and to trust that there are ways out of even the darkest rooms.

People cry out for a caring and protective God at their most extreme moments. A woman tells of how hysterical she became when she was about to be evicted from her apartment: "I said, 'Oh God, what am I going to do?' And I prayed and I cried, say, 'God, help me get through this.'" She believes that praying in this way mattered, for God helped show them the way to this shelter.

Similarly, a single woman living with her three children and two grandchildren reports a feeling of helplessness before they entered the shelter and met a woman there who helped them: "Before we got here, they were already down, wondering what's going to happen, where are we going? . . . 'Mama, what are we going to do?'" Realizing that she lacked the money to return home to the Midwest, she reports that she and her children turned to God: "And so we'd just pray, and ask the Lord to open a way, and he will, and so that's when I met Rita in the shelter."

Sometimes the view that God protects comes extremely close to denial that real suffering has occurred at all. A strongly committed Baptist woman responds pointedly to the suggestion that God might be letting her down by admitting that "I have had that feeling at one time, but I know that he would never let us suffer." Her time of doubt was related to a physical illness, but she has arrived back at a place of firmer faith: "When I found out that I had this lump in surgery, I thought that he was making me suffer, but I prayed every night, and I think he was making a way for us. I believe in him very much." Such statements present an odd Christian theology, of course, since they suggest that faith prevents suffering. But this response reveals the linkage between belief in God and the faith that God protects people from suffering.

Belief in God's protection can sometimes be interpreted as a more general orientation. One woman who refers to religion as "bigotry" insists that she believes in God "with all my heart, and I know God helped me, and he's helping me." She acknowledges that her situation could be worse: "I could be sick, my kids could be sick, and we could be on that beach [instead of in this shelter]. . . . God protects me. I know he has, and I know he always will. It's not so easy when things don't go right, there's a reason for it, it's a learning process, there's something. I don't understand why, but I know out of all of it, I'll get through it. I always have."

Similarly, a man views his present situation as a "mission" and a "quest" that God has placed him on in order to "build up strength within ourselves." God is "watching over us," and he attributes each event that might have turned out worse to God's presence and protection. God saved the life of his family years before by not allowing a bomb to explode that had been thrown through their window.

An even more dramatic story of transcendent intervention comes from a woman who was stabbed savagely by a man she was living with. She relates (in a somewhat amazed tone of voice) what happened to her during that episode:

> I wasn't very religious at the time, but I heard a voice say, "Ask the man for a hug." You're kidding! This man is stabbing on me, and you want me to give him a hug? I didn't question who was talking. . . . And I heard another cool calm voice say, "Give the man a hug, ask the man for a hug." Well, I don't know any other way out of this situation, so I said, "Will you give me a hug?" And the guy kind of snapped to reality again . . . and he said, "Let go of my arm." I had ahold of his arm with the knife in it. And I heard the voice say, "Trust him." . . . I said, okay. I let go of his arm. He dropped the knife, gave me a hug, took me to the hospital. I never asked, "Why me?" because I knew why me. . . . Down the road, I started pondering, "Who was speaking to me?"

She interprets this event according to the ideas of a religious movement focusing on miracles, and she believes that the voice she heard is her own guiding intuition.

But God can function as a protector in many subtle ways. For example, Darlene Martin, whose story we heard at the beginning of chapter 3, speaks proudly of her refusal to become a prostitute, linking this decision with her religious identity and faith: "I have a spiritual side of myself, and I believe in God, I believe in Jesus Christ, and also I believe he is my helper. So because of my spiritual background and my belief in God, that's what brought me through, and not to lower myself to a standard of money."

She delivers a long sermon-like explanation of her situation, making the following specific theological assertions: (1) if you don't do what God wants you to do, you "really can't rely on God protecting you and taking care of you"; (2) the Bible provides the basic guidelines people have to follow; (3) she has experienced both sides of God's presence and is convinced that if "I choose to be disobedient, I choose to live the way I wanted to and get off from the things I want to get off into, I reap what I sow"; (4) having chosen in that way, "I don't feel like God is responsible for where I'm at, I feel like my self is responsible for why I'm in [this situation]"; but (5) she has not "given up on God," and she still recognizes that God is really there although she is the one responsible for her own life.

An entire theology of suffering is implicit in these reflections. She sums up her present position by saying: "I believe that now that I'm here, I more or less relate to God on a sort of daily basis and to guide my life and get my life back into line with him. So that I can be led out with the peace of God in me, that I can be led out with the joy and peace of God in me, wherever I go, that I know I'm being led by God and not by myself. So that's my basic belief in God, that's all I know of God, and I study his word to understand it more." Ms. Martin is convinced that God's grace has brought her through her depression, at the same time insisting that her problems have been primarily her responsibility.

In another explanation of suffering, the responsibility for it is split, with God acting to protect us only when we take the first step. Such a view can be combined with a judgmental orientation, whereby the individual's guilt prevents God from helping us until we are ready. These are the views of a middle-aged woman who sees God as continually giving her "a way out," then waiting for her to take it. "But now that I did, he's making things look brighter and brighter for me." She is convinced that God is providing help to her gradually: "He's not going to just put it at my feet, he's giving it to me gradually so I can grasp the whole and see exactly what he's trying to show me."

God as Comforter

God may not be able (or even willing) to protect us from suffering and tragedy. But our faith may be able to comfort us throughout our experiences, if only by reminding us that we are not alone. One of the most common ways in which the homeless families in our study tried to make sense of their troubles was to hold onto the belief that God remained with them, even when he was not protecting them from terrible trials. For example, one woman says that she believes in God and sees him as support, placing the emphasis more on God's presence than on his explicit help: "Times are going to get bad for all of us, and we got to keep the faith, and keep the faith means we have to be strong, don't give up."

Comforting can be as simple and gentle as a sense of presence and positive feeling at the end of a difficult day. As one woman expresses it: "Sometimes when I feel so insecure, I pray to God to help me . . . to believe this and that. And sometimes I'll go to sleep and I'll suddenly wake up and I don't know what it is, and I'll go, 'Oh, maybe because I didn't pray.' I'll pray, and I'll feel better." For another troubled woman, the key is to remember that although "there will be trials and tribulations," God has said that "I won't give you any more than you can stand, so that's a relief."

The experience of God's comfort can also involve simply a sense that he is involved and will act somehow, whether or not it is to protect or save. We see this response most directly in the comments of Ms. Barbara Kelly at the beginning of this chapter, who puts her faith in Jesus and then just takes life as it comes. The difference between focusing on protection and focusing on comfort is revealed in the comments of a woman who says that "even down as far as I feel I have gone, I still feel that the Lord is taking care of us in there somewhere too. That's probably why I haven't totally fallen apart." She admits that "it's very easy to say, Why is God doing this to me?" But it is "a very humbling thing" to recognize that "there are people living here who are much worse off than I am." God does not protect her from experiencing pain or tragedy, but her awareness of God prevents her from falling apart in the midst of her problems.

A woman who was brought up in a religious family speaks simply about the centrality of prayer and faith: "As long as you believe and have the faith, things will work out." She recognizes that she cannot make it on her own: "You are going to always have problems, but these problems here is a little bit more difficult than anybody can handle."

But God's comfort can come in more dramatic ways. A woman whose son was drowned by a nephew was unable to forgive her sister for allowing this to happen until she had a powerful religious experience: "I was just laying there one night sleeping, and all my lights went out in my apartment, and there was just like a glow, and there was my son standing there, and he told me, said I must forgive and forget and must make up with my sister, I must go out because he wouldn't want this, it's just like a disturbance to him. And I made amends with her, I went and talked."

Belief in God's comforting presence can also make sense of suffering by providing a baseline beyond which no harm can really matter. A woman who has cancer reports in a calm and almost detached tone of voice: "Death to me will be a beautiful day. . . . I'm not afraid to die. I've never let that bother me one bit." She teaches her children to pray and believes that God provides answers that help her deal with life: "You're walking down the street, and all of a sudden there's an answer." She insists that "the good Lord's going to guide us, and that's that." What has happened to her is her responsibility, not God's, but God has "always been there" for her in the worst times, "and it's been open for me, I just have to reach out and get it." The "it" is not so much protection or even guidance, but a presence, a sense of God upholding and comforting her family. There is a deep element of humility in her attitude, evinced by her comment that "He gave his only begotten son for us, so who am I?" Who am I to deny God's presence, and who am I to feel that I don't deserve that presence?

God as Justifier

While we may not believe that God protects us from bad experiences or even comforts us in the midst of our suffering, we might still believe that God will somehow cause everything to come out all right in the end, even if it takes another life to reveal that to us. For example, one homeless person reports that God's caring means that she will eventually be helped in some way: "I feel like when I die I'm going to heaven, because I'm not that bad of a—I'm not no, what do you call them people who go to church four times a week and do wrong four times a week?—hypocrite, I'm not a hypocrite."

Two related cognitive moves are apparent in this statement. She is assured that she will go to heaven, and thus that her suffering is not permanent. But also (and perhaps more significant), she can believe that what is happening to her is not really her fault because God will not punish her for being as bad as a hypocrite. She has done her best, she has tried her hardest, and that is all God can expect from her.

God may also justify our suffering by redeeming it. One woman repeatedly tells herself that "maybe right now I'm going through all of this, maybe God's getting me prepared for [when I am] older where I have everything that I possibly might want." Her mother used to tell her that when you have problems, you just have to keep going; God is carrying you and all of your troubles.

An even clearer statement of this viewpoint comes from a woman who regularly talks to God and admits to him that she doesn't know why she is going through all of this turmoil. But she is convinced that "I'm going through this for something. I don't know what it is yet, but maybe it's to make me a better person, or to make me more sensitive to other people." When her husband asks her why their children are also suffering, her response is, "Hey, it's going to make them stronger adults."

A woman who shares this view repeatedly defines her homelessness as a "learning experience" that God is putting them through for the sake of other people: "I've never been in this situation before, but once I know we're going to get out of it and we're going for it, once we make it we can help other people, we can help somebody else." When her husband became depressed about his inability to provide for them, she replied that "this is an experience that God wanted us to go through, and this is his way of showing us how to make it through, this is a learning experience."

Another way in which suffering can be justified is in recognizing that God is ultimately in control of it. A shelter resident struggling to understand what has been happening to her tries to maintain a balance between utter pessimism and unrealistic optimism. Her solution is to trust that God must be involved in the process somewhere, and therefore she cannot—indeed, she must not—try to control or understand what is happening: "I don't ever really get my hopes up too high, because I have so many disappointments as it was.... Just keep trying, keep looking, something eventually's going to turn up.... I said, 'Well Lord, I'm just going to turn in the hands to you, because I can't seem, I tried to do it on my own, I just get failure after failure. I'm going to just put it in your hands. If it's for me, I know you'll give it to me. If not, I know it's not for me.' "

She also believes that part of the purpose of suffering is to move to the point of acknowledging her dependence on God: "Some things, he'll allow some things to happen before, for you to realize that he is God." She believes that "everything is done for a purpose" and that God "will turn the devil on you, but he won't let him destroy your life.... The main thing is to have enough faith."

Another homeless mother uses the image of testing in relation to God's ability to redeem human suffering:

> When I get mad, sometimes, I say, "AAHHH, why'd you do this to me?!" But I feel that God's there, he's there. Right now we're all being tested to see how we can handle things, and it's just like truth or consequences, you do something and every single day you're going to make a decision that's going to affect the rest of your life, I don't care what it is.... Everything we do is our decision... that's ours, that's not God who's making you do it, that's us. I feel like, if you get in a jam and you need the help, you can call on him and ask for help.

A single father is committed to his faith that "with Jesus Christ on your side, can you lose?" He attributes his beliefs to his mother, who helped him to see that God is the greatest "ally" a person can have. When he considers the troubles he and his daughter have had, he falls back on his belief that God is trying to remind him of what is truly important and that their suffering therefore is serving God's higher purpose: "I understand why He's doing it.... It's bringing me back to reality, remember who you are, where you're from, what is real and what isn't real." Reality for him involves being wrenched out of the everyday material world, and the proof of this perspective is the course his own life has taken: "I've had realty, I've had a number of cars, I've had seven cars at one time, I've had rental property, I've had bank accounts and things of this nature, and everything I had I worked for. And I lost it all, I've lost it all." The loss of everything is a sign, not that God has deserted him, but rather that God is revealing something new and unexpected to him.

Suffering can also be justified in terms of some hidden purpose. For example, a woman raised in a nonreligious household insists that her problems are her responsibility, not God's. Saying that "I don't think God makes problems, I think we made them all ourselves," she goes on to admit that it would be nice to live in a world where pain and suffering disappeared. But she is chastened enough about her own life to accept the disappointments and losses on their own terms: "So therefore I'll have to live with what I have to live with. And there's times when I'll say, 'Yeah, that's too rough. Hey, Lord, can you make it a little easier?' But I'm not going to say that God's punishing me." When asked whether she doesn't feel sometimes that God is indeed punishing her, she replies: "Well, sometimes, but then again everybody feels that way—but the thing is, I think if there's no bad times there'll be no good times. You have to take the bad with the good. Because the bad times show what kind of strength you have. If it's always good, you don't know what kind of strength you have. Everybody can deal with it nice, but how many people can deal with it rough?"

Struggling with Meaning

We do not want to give the impression that all homeless people are content with the answers they have found in their search to make sense of their (and their children's) problems. Some of them continue to ask the age-old questions of how a good and powerful God can allow such awful things to happen to people.

One woman who still prays, "but not as much as I'd like to," admits that she has often questioned whether God exists, and she tells us nervously that her husband is an atheist. She is particularly troubled by the suffering of her children: "I ask the good Lord why, all the time.... You don't understand why the good Lord don't just say, 'Hey, I haven't forgotten about you.'" Another woman admits that, particularly when she first became homeless, she found herself asking, "Why me? Why is this happening to me?...I haven't done nothing to nobody, and this happening to me."

The apparent success of other people who seem to be living more immoral lives can be galling to someone whose life is falling apart. One woman says she finds herself asking God why "all the things bad has happened to me, and I don't know, a lot of bad people and they don't have nothing to them." Another woman admits to her confusion when she reflects about her present attitudes about religion: "I just wonder sometime why is this so hard? Just to make ends meet. Because it's been times, I always tried to be Mrs. Goody Two-Shoes, do things straight down the line as far as the law would and everything, but then you look at someone else, they're breaking all the laws and they have more than you have, and it gets you down."

Conclusion

We should not be surprised that so many homeless families continue to try to find meaning in their experiences, nor is it surprising that religious belief provides a context for such questioning. The sociological reality is that traditional religious beliefs remain prevalent in American society. In addition, we must remember that one of the major functions of religious reflection and religious communities has been to "comfort the afflicted," providing at least tentative ways to understand one's life as connected to some sort of higher purpose.

The reasons for asking questions on the meaning of life are tied to the basic elements of human dignity discussed earlier. To become aware that we have lost the capacity to choose leads us to ask who, in fact, is in control, and why we have been deprived of this basic right to make decisions for ourselves. To see everything as chaotic and unpredictable drives us to search for something understandable, stable, and constant in the midst of the terror and flux of our daily lives. To be stifled in expressing or living out who we feel ourselves to be—and to be cut off from the community that used to give our lives coherence—pushes us to ask deeper questions about the self, and about the community of faith or meaning that seems so hidden by our current alienation and isolation.

But is there room for concern about a "higher purpose" in the lives of people who are worried about where their next meal is coming from, or where their children will be sleeping next week? This is the wrong question to ask. People do ask about that purpose, and they will continue to understand their experiences in terms of some meaning (whether religious or not) that allows them to transcend their daily suffering.

What we have discovered in the musings and reflections of most of the adults we interviewed is that their sense of who they are as persons is tied to making sense of their lives. In this way, as in so many others, they are very much like the rest of us. Their capacity to understand their lives as meaningful, or at least to continue to search for such an understanding, stands at the very heart of their insistence that they remain human beings capable of, and committed to, being actors and adults on a grander stage than the cot on which they are sleeping each night. The hope they have to retain and recreate some of their dignity rests precisely on continuing to search for such meaning, whether or not they find it.

Indeed, it is not surprising that both the Jewish and Christian traditions have used the images of homelessness in describing the fundamental condition of human life. Biblical language is replete with the imagery of the stranger, the wanderer, the pilgrim, and the outcast. Judaism has always placed particular emphasis on the longing for the land that has been lost, on the experience of being a "stranger in a strange land." And Christianity has often emphasized the ways in which our true situation (if we could only recognize it) is one of a community of pilgrims living in a world that is not really our own.

Perhaps people who are in such dire straits as homeless families are can confront the inner truths of these religious traditions more easily than the rest of us. After all, questions of theodicy are not academic exercises in their lives. Similarly, the struggle of alienated creatures to find some point of connection and loyalty in the midst of a strange and confusing world resonates fully with their day-to-day experiences. It is not surprising that so many of them find religious beliefs and values to be such important resources.

PART FOUR

Moral Reflections

7

The Concept
of Dignity

Homelessness can be understood from many different perspectives: as a social problem, threatening the stability and economy of American society; as a psychological problem, threatening the mental and emotional health of a segment of the population; or as an aesthetic problem, undermining the quality of life in American cities. All these perspectives are important, and none of them can be ignored. But in this chapter, in particular, our focus is on homelessness as a moral problem, raising concerns about the basic rights and responsibilities human beings have and express toward one another. From this viewpoint, being homeless threatens the essential dignity of human beings, undermining and often destroying their ability to be seen, and to see themselves, as worthwhile persons.

When we speak about the most fundamental and important aspects of human life, we often find ourselves focusing on self-respect and personal dignity as being the basepoints against which we evaluate the behavior of others as well as our own actions. There are many tragedies in life, but when someone compromises their self-respect or loses their dignity as a human being, we are often moved to declare that something very fundamental has gone awry. In extreme circumstances, such as those in concentration camps, it is not only the physical torture or deprivation that troubles us, but the breaking of a person's spirit—the fact that the inner attitude, the essential person, is destroyed. It is the reduction of a person to purely physical circumstances that represents the greatest threat to the moral order.

Dignity is that element of the self and human spirit that is separable from our possessions, our jobs, our physical appearance, and our abilities. Dignity is something deeper than these material factors. It refers to the moral center of the person. In the words of Peter Berger: "Dignity, as against honor, always relates to the intrinsic humanity divested of all socially imposed roles or norms. It pertains to the self as such, to the individual regardless of his position in society."[1] Dignity directs our attention to the inner person, to the fundamental aspects of personhood.

From the perspective of the individual, dignity is an expression of one's intentionality toward the world. Dignity is threatened when one merely mirrors circumstances rather than acting upon them. People who can experience their lives in terms of dignity, however restricted their environment and choices, are nevertheless pursuing a life project: their interpretations of the world reflect their intentionality toward the future. They have plans. People without dignity, in contrast, are individuals without a future, without a project, without hope. They act (or, at least, are perceived) as passive victims who have relinquished their lives to someone else or to circumstances they deem beyond their control.

To act with dignity, to be aware of oneself as intrinsically valuable, can be experienced as a moral imperative. It is what defines one's essential humanity. Equally essential, however, is the right of all human beings to be treated with dignity—in other words, to relate to them in a manner that allows them to have an inner attitude, a world of dreams and hopes and intentions toward the future. To attack the dignity of others is to treat them as if they merely mirror their circumstances, as if they accept others' interpretations of their lives and are subject to other peoples' agendas.

Religious, Philosophical, and Legal Views of Dignity

To raise the question of whether we are to be treated with dignity is to raise one of the most fundamental questions of human life: Are we in fact worthwhile, valuable, simply by virtue of the fact that we exist? Several of the dominant philosophical and religious traditions of the West have addressed this question and have developed elaborate ways to answer in the affirmative. For example, claims about human rights are dependent upon some underlying presupposition of the essential dignity of every human being, apart from the status or role any person occupies. To assert a claim as a human right, in other words, is to insist that, simply because I am a human being, I should be treated in certain ways, or at least I should not be deprived of the opportunity to act in certain ways.

In the twentieth century one can identify a growing awareness in the international community of the importance of human rights language and appeals, in spite of the myriad ways in which human societies fall short of the ideal. To cite only one influential example, the Universal Declaration of Human Rights (adopted by the United Nations General Assembly in 1948) begins by stating in its preamble that "recognition of the inherent dignity and of the equal and inalienable rights of all members of the human family is the foundation of freedom, justice and peace in the world." The declaration goes on in Article 1 to state: "All human beings are born free and equal in dignity and rights." A host of later documents make the same point, insisting that there is something fundamental about the very concept of dignity that links it to the notion of rights and thereby to the way in which societies should be organized and individuals protected. The central insight is that there is some inherent worth in all persons, and this fact requires certain sorts of responses from others.[2]

American society in the 1990s has a tendency to adopt an extremely individualistic and confrontational understanding of human rights. A right is usually perceived as something individuals possess, to which they can appeal when they are treated in a certain way. It is worth noting that much of the earlier religious tradition out of which rights language develops had a much more social, and even species-specific, understanding of the basis of human dignity. The central concept in the biblical understanding of human nature, for example, begins with the view that human beings are created in God's image, an idea that gives an essential compelling dignity to all human life. Even most of the strands of the Christian tradition that stressed the importance of the fallenness of human beings continued to recognize our underlying divine image, which was effaced, but not erased, in the course of human history.[3] The precise content or interpretation of that divine image has been a subject of heated debate, but the central claim has continued to be made: namely, that human beings have intrinsic value, not because of what they do or who they become, but because they mirror and carry some reflection of the source of ultimate value. And in spite of the particularism and narrowness that has all-too-often infected Jewish and Christian understandings of history, the center of both traditions leads back to the insistence that all human beings share this essential component of the divine image.[4]

To provide still another related example, Western philosophical thought has been enormously influenced by the importance placed by Immanuel Kant (at the end of the eighteenth century) on the dignity of the human being. For Kant, the essential feature of human moral life is autonomy, and his ethical approach centers around the absolute command to treat all people as ends rather than only as means. As we shall see, autonomy may be overemphasized, but it is clear that Kant is pointing to the same underlying insight of the intrinsic worth of the human being. Whether we focus our attention on the capacity for moral reasoning, individual choice, interpersonal compassion, or some other understanding, there is a surprising consensus in our religious and philosophical traditions concerning a dignity in human life that is independent of any of the vagaries or accidents of social standing or personal action. There is an inner worth that is to be acknowledged, respected, and acted upon.

But as we indicated earlier, although dignity refers to our inner worth, it remains something that is both internally experienced and externally validated. I truly "have" dignity only if two conditions are met: I must view and carry myself with dignity, and other people must respond to me as possessing dignity. If only the former condition is met, my dignity can be neither recognized nor validated, leading to the suspicion that among other people it is not, indeed, dignity at all. On the other hand, if only the latter condition is met, I will not be able to experience myself in terms of how others view me, a discrepancy that leads to inner uncertainty and self-doubt.

Thus, there is a delicate balance between the subjective and objective sides of dignity. Precisely because the views of other people help to define and reinforce our own subjective experience of ourselves as worthwhile, there is always a social and "situated" aspect of dignity, if the term is not to dissolve into the ethereal world of utterly abstract claims. I always experience my dignity in terms of my life as it exists, and this means as a member of this society, of this community, and of this era. Common elements comprise that dignity across all such contexts, but I can only experience it within a given context. Michael Walzer points in this direction when he writes, concerning the importance of self-respect in democratic societies:

> It is the minimal standards intrinsic to the practice of democracy that set the norms of self-respect. And as these standards spread throughout civil society, they make possible a kind of self-respect that isn't dependent on any particular social position, that has to do with one's general standing in the community and with one's sense of oneself, not as a person simply but as a person effective in such and such a setting, a full and equal member, an active participant. . . .
>
> Self-respect requires, then, some substantial connection to the group of members, to the movement that champions the idea of professional honor, class solidarity, or citizen rights, or to the larger community within which these ideas are more or less well established.[5]

We believe that what Walzer writes of self-respect can be applied to our discussion of dignity. It is logically possible to claim that someone has dignity even if no others affirm it or to claim that my experience of my own dignity is sufficient. But dignity is an essentially social and interactive term. Dignity implies a conferral of a particular status or set of rights, not only by oneself but also by others. To say someone is dignified, or possesses dignity, is to make a social, as well as a psychological, statement.[6]

The application of such a concept to the experiences of homeless persons should be quite obvious. We are concerned about how homeless people experience their own intrinsic sense of dignity, how other people and institutions treat them as people with dignity, and how homeless people uphold their own dignity in the midst of their experiences. These issues tell us something not only about the homeless, but about America's actual, lived-out values as well. If it is true that we can best learn about a society by looking at the people in it who are the most disadvantaged, then examining the question of the dignity of the homeless may be an appropriate starting point for learning about how (and, indeed, whether) we truly believe that all persons deserve to be treated in certain ways.

Listening to the voices of the homeless provides us with an important and revealing insight into the central values of American society. Stripped of most of the standard trappings of status and role, the homeless confront us with troubling questions. Do we truly value and respect people for their own sakes? Is the worth of a person determined by place of residence, occupation, or income?

If dignity is dependent solely on our being human, it should not be affected by our material situation or our social status. But we experience dignity through our own self-image and the way we are treated by others. If I view myself as someone who is worthless, and if others treat me in that way, my dignity has been significantly threatened, whether or not I believe, at a deeper philosophical level, that I continue to have dignity. Dignity not experienced is, too often, dignity denied.

Conditions for Dignity among Homeless Families

The term "dignity" was not frequently used by the homeless families we interviewed. But in listening to parents tell their stories of how they became homeless and their struggle to find housing for themselves and their families, the subtext in many of these narratives was the threat they felt to their humanity—their personhood. In probing their descent into home-lessness and their interaction with welfare workers, shelter personnel, and people they encountered in their efforts to find housing, what seemed to be at stake was whether they were treated with dignity and whether, personally, they were able to continue to relate to their own circumstances with a sense of dignity.

Drawing on the foregoing discussion of the concept of dignity, what is at stake for homeless people is whether they are seen by others, and whether they view themselves, as being "selves" independent of their circumstances. The distinguishing mark of whether other people treated them with dignity was whether they acknowledged that a homeless person was capable of relating to their circumstances with intentionality. Were they viewed simply as a victim of bad circumstances, poor judgment, and inadequate financial management, or were they viewed as someone capable of having a future, of imagining a project for their life and their children? As long as homeless persons are viewed simply as victims, then social service workers, and even those involved in philanthropic efforts, may relate to them in impersonal, problem-solving ways that deny their humanity.

In closely examining the life narratives of the interviewees, we have identified four factors that figure significantly in the experience of dignity by homeless people. They are autonomy, predictability, self-expression, and social solidarity with a community. These four factors are the basis for living life with dignity.

Different people will experience each of these conditions in various ways. We are not suggesting that all of these elements are always necessary, nor that they are the only ways to think about the maintenance of dignity. In addition, many of these conditions are highly culture-specific; for example, the importance of autonomy reveals the continuing influence of Kantian thought on the way Americans tend to understand what is ultimately important about their lives. We do believe, however, that these are fundamental factors that provide our citizens with a recognition of the dignity both of others and of themselves. In identifying them, we begin to understand the ways in which homelessness both undercuts the experience of dignity and creates the need to reassert that dignity in different ways.

Autonomy

The most important condition of dignity is an appropriate degree of autonomy. Human beings require a sphere of choice, a sphere of action over which they have some control and discretion. To be marched through daily tasks, fed from predetermined menus and on predetermined schedules, constrained in whom you speak to and how you spend your time, and prevented from making any decisions to alter the next steps you may take—such restrictions undermine the humanity that we usually assume separates us from other animate or inanimate beings. To be a human being is to be capable of making choices; to severely restrict our choices is to threaten our human dignity.

To expect autonomy over my life means that I want, or demand, to be viewed not merely as someone who makes choices, but as someone who is able to make them. To deprive someone of that autonomy must, therefore, be justified on the grounds that the person is not able to make choices. When we make such a judgment responsibly, we must be prepared to make the case as to why a particular individual is incapable of being granted autonomy over some area of life.

In many situations, of course, such justifications are readily apparent. Parents can view children as lacking judgment and physical or emotional maturity, and social institutions (such as families and courts) are often given the power to limit choice-making by the mentally ill or morally irresponsible. But the most complex and compelling arguments about social policy arise precisely when we are trying to decide how valid such arguments are.

For example, how capable are persons with certain mental illnesses of making decisions about their own lives? Most legal jurisdictions in our society allow people to be hospitalized against their will only if they are seen to be a danger to themselves or to others. Even if this standard is agreed upon, it is often easier to define than to apply. Am I a danger to myself if I am unable to make decisions that appear to others to be in my self-interest? How much leeway should I be allowed before my decisions are constrained? All of us would doubtless agree that there are some things I could do that would indicate that the line has been crossed, but precisely where is that line?

Human beings grow into autonomy; we would not criticize a parent for laying down rules for a young child or disciplining that child, because we recognize that freedom assumes certain qualities of judgment and ability. Indeed, to be granted autonomy by others means that we are viewed as individuals who possess the requisite degree of judgment and ability to make decisions that will affect both our own lives and those around us.

Autonomy is multidimensional, and there may be strong arguments for limiting choice in certain areas without thereby completely undermining someone's sense of control over life. The specifics of the situation are always important, and the lines are difficult to draw. We are probably better off viewing such types of limitations as falling along a continuum, and each of us will have our own way of ordering those limitations.

For example, consider the following four limits on autonomy, which are often experienced by the homeless families we interviewed as conditions for residing in shelters: (1) their welfare and homeless aid checks are held by the shelters, to be returned upon the end of the two-month stay; (2) they must not stay in the shelters during the day; (3) no cooking is allowed in most shelter rooms; and (4) strict curfews on children and parents are enforced.

Some of these restrictions can be justified for safety reasons. But others (such as keeping the checks) seem based more on an assumption that these families are too irresponsible to save their money without being coerced into doing so. The force of this latter restriction is softened somewhat by the fact that staying in the shelter is itself voluntary—and, indeed, highly sought after in most instances. But the practice does reinforce a view that these parents do not have to be treated as adults. Whether or not we agree with the practice (and most of the families do agree with it), its negative effect on autonomy remains.

It is less important to draw precise lines than it is to recognize the importance of such limitations on homeless families. When our lives are severely constrained, we are less able to view ourselves as moving through our own world, as influencing what happens to ourselves and to others. When the decisions are made by other institutional authorities, with no input or counsel from us, our inner sense of dignity is threatened.

At the same time, such restrictions undermine the way in which we are viewed by others. In the case of homeless parents, their relatives, friends, and acquaintances begin to view them as helpless, as unable to take care of themselves. Perhaps most significant, their children begin to view them in that way as well. We heard repeated statements from parents about how proud they were that their children were taking care of *them,* supporting and nurturing them in the midst of their turmoil. While such stories are inspiring, they are also troubling because the reversal of the traditional relationship between parent and child undermines the parent's sense of responsibility and the child's sense of security. Without autonomy residing in the appropriate sphere, family relationships become strained and unclear.

In short, to acknowledge autonomy as an essential aspect of human dignity is to place the burden squarely on those who would limit choice. The burden can be borne in many situations, and we should not be afraid to make the argument when we are convinced that certain people cannot be allowed to act for themselves. But our legal system responds to a deep-seated moral imperative when it hedges such limitations with both procedural and substantive restrictions before allowing either individuals or social institutions to undercut the ways in which people can make decisions for themselves.

We would readily acknowledge that the focus on autonomy can go too far and that American society may often be criticized precisely for overemphasizing the value of independence. From a religious perspective, for example, the recognition of ultimate dependence is critical; indeed, it might even be said that the most basic distinction between a religious and nonreligious worldview has to do with whether or not one recognizes an ultimate dependence on something other than either self or society. Similarly, the priority often given to competitive over cooperative values reminds us of the dangers of ignoring the ways in which we are continually dependent upon one another in all aspects of our lives. The political arguments between liberals, conservatives, and libertarians can be understood as disputes over precisely where to draw the lines on this value conflict; but virtually no one denies that there is such a line, and that some actions lie on one side and some on the other.

For our purposes, it is sufficient to remember that homeless people are likely to be all too aware of the extent of their dependence upon others. It is at best overstated, and at worst insensitive, to tell them simply to accept the inevitability of mutual dependence or to remind them that we are all confronted with limited choices. At some point, the degree of limited choice becomes a qualitatively different reality, and we must be willing to imagine what it would be like to have our choices constrained so dramatically and comprehensively.

When we look at homeless people, it is often tempting to justify helping them by using analogies that all-too-easily undercut the value of autonomy in their lives. If we believe they are homeless because they have been unable to make adult decisions about their own lives, we may slide into viewing them as children and thus justify telling them what to do and how to solve their problems. Similarly, if we view them as morally irresponsible or lazy, our response may resemble the approach taken to criminals or sociopaths, whose lack of social responsibility justifies severe constraints.

As we saw in chapter 2, however, people become homeless for many reasons, and it is almost always possible to find elements of irresponsibility and poor judgment in their lives (just as it would be possible to do so in our own, of course). This is precisely why it is so important, particularly when discussing the lives of people who are disadvantaged and marginalized, to begin by asserting the value of autonomy as something they possess merely by virtue of being human beings.

One common result of the loss of autonomy is the sense of individual passivity. Life has become a story of things happening to them; they are no longer actors, no longer decision-makers. In chapter 2 we heard Mrs. Hernandez describe herself as someone who needs to become "more aggressive in life, because I think this has caused me a lot of problems, just sitting back and relaxing." Similar comments are found in many interviews we conducted.

This passivity stems from an understanding of the new pressures on their lives. We might become passive because we don't need to act or because we are tired of acting; for these homeless families, however, passivity seems to be the most reasonable response to living in a world they can no longer fathom or affect. Recall Betty Reynold's attempts to save herself and her children when her problems became acute. She responded to her daughter's drug use by withholding money, only to be confronted with broken windows and a violent man. Her efforts to move to a more stable location broke down when a relative's friend proved to be unreliable, and her last-ditch efforts to stay in a motel foundered on insufficient money and the motel's location in a dangerous neighborhood.

The lack of autonomy that homeless people feel is found in the most concrete arenas of life. The loss of a home robs them of the physical protection and privacy associated with a secure and autonomous existence. Protection is expressed in terms of the desire to have "a roof over our heads," a haven for dealing with the world. Life in the shelter provides some of that protection, as expressed most clearly by the woman who told us that finding the shelter was the best thing that had happened to her recently. She now feels she can take a walk with her son, knowing she has somewhere to come back to; she can "take a shower and lay my head, and my baby got a roof over his head, and he's got formula and he can eat."

Autonomy comes in various forms, and none of us is immune to experiencing and regretting its absence. Its significance was indicated most poignantly by an exchange between an eight-year-old girl and her seven-year-old brother, talking about what it felt like to have slept in a car for a month. The girl says, "It was rough, every time I went to sleep, my brother always kept on putting his feet up to my face!" Her brother responds, "That's because I didn't have nowhere else to put them!"

Predictability

The second condition for dignity is that we enjoy some degree of predictability about our future. People often lose control of their lives not because they are weak or incompetent but because the world around them stops making sense. In other words, not only have these people lost their bearings, but—from their perspective—the social world has lost *its* bearings. Predictability is an attribute applied not only to other people but to the world at large, and it is precisely this broader attribution which has been undercut.

Living in a predictable world is essential to sensing that we are functioning in a social world, and thus to our self-image as responsible adults. Without the capacity to live in a world that we can act upon and affect in predictable ways, we are unable to follow through, to make plans, to act as people whose decisions have effects on others. It is not surprising, therefore, that when our lives are too chaotic and open-ended, we feel impotent, which in turn makes it even harder to act forcefully to escape from the chaos.

Predictability is also essential if we are to have a life project. A whole and fulfilling human life can only be understood in terms of having a life project: namely, some pattern of concerted activities that we choose and live out. The project can encompass virtually any human activity: developing a career track within an organization, pursuing a creative hobby, raising children, doing volunteer work in a church. Projects can be interlocking and can alter as we grow and find new interests. Whatever their specific content, projects define us as human beings capable of having concerns, of planning and pursuing them, willing to work and "project" ourselves into the future.

One reason why having a project is so important for human beings is that it allows us to become (and to be seen as) consistent actors. Defined in terms of my ongoing project, I have a solidity, an ability to be the same person from one day to the next, a focus behind all the myriad activities in which I am engaged. Even when I am not aware that I do have a life project, my sense of self is affected by the broader and ongoing activities in which I continue to participate. By doing so, I become someone who has a center, who acts.

Once again, we can adopt too narrow an understanding of life projects, and the American tendency to view being active as intrinsically valuable may result in a dismissive attitude to any project that does not look like a typical career or line of accomplishment. We would insist that focusing on the centrality of a project need not bias us against giving full and deserved weight to the more passive aspects of a full human life. Indeed, part of what is necessary is to redefine our understanding of "work," to remind ourselves that reimbursed employment or outward creativity represents only one form of human work.[7] Our projects are defined much more subjectively than most of us might want to admit, and the value of activities such as waiting and attending needs to be reaffirmed. The point remains, however, that if dignity depends on the possibility of having a life project, being homeless can undermine that possibility.

To live in a thoroughly unpredictable world destroys the possibility of having a life project. There are never any guarantees in life, of course, for any of us; but it is hard to imagine focusing our energies on any ongoing activity without at least a reasonable degree of faith that what we do today will be relevant and in place tomorrow. Indeed, it is hard to imagine what our lives would be like once the assumption of predictability is completely shaken. We could make no commitments or promises, either to activities or to other persons; we could develop no interests, take no risks, invest in no training. All the activities and interests that define human persons would dissolve once we learned the lesson that what happens to us is random, that the stability of the natural and social world cannot be counted on at all. If we believe that this sense of having a project is a central dimension in the lives of all human beings, we can understand the threat to human dignity posed by the destruction of predictability.

The desire to regain a sense of predictability can become an all-consuming obsession for a parent staring at a homeless child. One of the mothers we interviewed focuses on providing her children with a different type of life in the midst of the instability, and she speaks of her compelling desire to alter the sense of the world that has been closing in on them: "I wanted mainly . . . to give the kids some kind of stability to go right on and get in church, so they'll know that at least this is one stable point in their life. And that's my goal, to get things back to normal as much as possible. I think the most shaking thing to them [was] the first earthquake that they ever felt." The church represents stability, the earthquake unpredictability. She even reports that one of her children is now extremely nervous about future earthquakes, reflecting his all-too-appropriate understanding of how shaky their lives are.

Predictability is also crucial to believing that our actions have some effect upon the wider social world. Human beings are often defined in terms of their ability to alter their environment, to understand and affect what is happening around them. Modern science depends upon the belief that there is some order in the natural world, that objects and relationships can be measured and defined, and that we are not living in a world that is completely random and fluid.

Even those of us who believe in a transcendent reality order our lives around certain expectations of consistency and dependability. This need for predictability is a basic human requirement for any ongoing individual or social existence. For example, societies that placed much more emphasis on magic believed that they could influence the workings of the universe or the gods by performing rituals and ceremonies. Belief in prayer can be another way in which societies structure their faith that whoever or whatever controls our fates is not completely arbitrary but at least is open to being influenced by heartfelt requests or self-sacrifice.

Certain forms of mental illness result from an unrealistic assessment of the unpredictability of human life. But we should not be too certain that what is unrealistic is always readily apparent. When we listen to the accounts of most of the homeless persons in our study, we are loathe to conclude that they are being unrealistic when they speak of the unpredictability of their lives. When events seem to conspire against us, when our best efforts seem to yield nothing but further disappointments, and when our only positive experiences arise from the sudden and unexpected actions of strangers or institutions, is it any wonder that our sense of a coherent and dependable social world disappears?

Self-Expression

As our discussion of the importance of having a life project suggests, experiencing dignity depends also upon opportunities for self-expression: the ability to express who we are and what we feel. As human beings, we are not merely free to act as we choose, we are also capable of expressing a range of emotions and attitudes toward ourselves and others, channeling that freedom in particular ways and with particular results. When such opportunities no longer exist, we become robots going through the motions, responding to either internal automatic responses or to external stimuli, with no intervening sense of a self acting in and through such events.

We might be tempted to say that these homeless people do indeed have an ongoing project: namely, to survive and provide for their children. But this viewpoint misses the key element of creation, which makes a project something more than simply a set of repeated actions. To build, support, and nourish one's children does not mean simply avoiding starvation or serious illness; if it is to become the focus for a human life, it must also involve coping with challenges in a creative and open way.

The test of whether our activities constitute a project is whether we can feel some degree of pride, self-respect, or self-worth in what we have done. The homeless parents in our interviews were left only with the satisfaction of having somehow fed or housed their children, usually by relying on helpful strangers or social institutions to provide the assistance. But they found it difficult to plan ahead, to feel that they were responding to the situation in a creative way, or to ensure that the assistance would be available next month or next year. When luck becomes the major explanation for feeding one's children, any sense of accomplishment or self-respect is likely to disappear.

It is difficult to identify this element of dignity, but it remains essential. For example, think about the experience of passing two homeless people on the street. One person walks haltingly, mumblingly asks us for money, averts his gaze from ours. The second person stands upright, speaks directly and clearly, looks us in the eye. We may know nothing about these two people, but our reaction to them is different. While we may be more or less compassionate, or more or less comfortable, with either one, the second person is more likely to elicit from us a feeling of respect, as if we can recognize a person in the tattered clothes and street context.

We hear similar reactions when people speak of the dignity represented by people coping with harsh treatment in other oppressive situations. When we see or hear images of Jewish people organizing and praying in concentration camps during World War II, we gain that same sense of dignity in the face of adversity. When we hear the stories of black men and women stoically carrying on in the midst of restrictive laws or hostile crowds, we recognize a strength of self in those people in spite of the limitations on their actions. Something shines through—an inner capacity, a deep awareness of who they are and what they can be.

Homeless families are forced to rely primarily on internal resources to maintain a sense of dignity. It would be extremely difficult for any of us to carry ourselves in that way even in the best of circumstances, without both a history of positive experiences and a continuing social system that reinforced our sense that we were worthwhile human beings. When we add the set of particularly disastrous experiences these families have just been through, we can understand how difficult it is for them to maintain a sense of inner dignity and to act out of that sense in front of others.

We must also acknowledge, on the basis of their own accounts, that many members of homeless families entered their present turmoil with extremely low self-esteem and terrible personal histories. In our study, reports were rampant of physical or sexual abuse in family relationships and of drug and alcohol abuse. Homeless people are not drawn randomly from the population; although their stories are unique and diverse, they are people who, by definition, have been living on the margins just before they became homeless. If they had viable support systems, money in the bank, good job opportunities, and excellent interpersonal skills, they would be extremely unlikely to find themselves on the streets or in shelters. To live on the margins is hard enough; to do so in the midst of a relatively wealthy and successful society is even more debilitating to our sense of self.

Social Solidarity

In addition to fostering autonomy, predictability, and self-expression, having a place to live also provides a deeper conviction that we are social beings worthy of being part of a community, adults who can take care of ourselves and fit into American society. To experience myself as a person with dignity, I must believe that I am in fact a worthwhile individual, however I may understand it. While we may believe that all persons deserve to be treated with dignity merely by virtue of the fact that they are human beings, most of us require some continual reassurances, some signs from others that we are in fact worthy of being treated in such a manner. As we argued above, dignity is validated both internally and externally; if all my experiences seem to send me the message that I am helpless and incompetent, and I live in a society that values independence and accomplishment, it would be surprising if I viewed myself as a worthy and responsible adult.

The greatest damage to homeless adults, particularly those with dependent children, may be an undermining of the sense that they are competent and worthwhile parents. The saddest comments are often comparative ones, when people look backward to the stability they used to have and forward to what they hope to have again. The present intervening chaos is thus revealed as a challenge not merely to comfort or happiness but to the story of their lives they wish to be able to tell. We hear in their voices not merely a frustration at having failed in the role of parent, but a broader challenge to their self-worth as human beings. Particularly for so many of the women we interviewed, whose sense of self was intimately tied up with their children or marriages, failures in these arenas represented a deeper failure in life.

People tell detailed stories of what they had accomplished in their lives before they became homeless, such as the woman who had painted her apartment and gathered praise from her neighbors for doing an excellent job. Being homeless deprives her not only of the roof over her head, but of the opportunity to demonstrate her talents and the seriousness of purpose in maintaining something of which she can be proud.

We hear such fears in the words of a depressed mother: "I have this daughter of mine, I can't even have a roof over her head. I should just give her up to somebody else that can take care of her, because it makes me feel inadequate. It feels like I'm not doing a good enough job being mom." The "job" is a socially defined one, and she is unable to take her place in that social world as "mom."

What is particularly crucial here is the social dimension of this need to see ourselves as worthy and responsible human beings. The interviews with homeless family members revealed not only threats to individual control and security but threats to feelings of social solidarity. In one respect, this is simply the other side of freedom or autonomy: namely, the capacity to make something of one's life, to rejoin society, to "be somebody" and to be recognized as such. For a parent, for example, being unable to provide for your children is a social statement that you are unfit for the role of parent.

More broadly, however, this more social dimension involves the need to make a contribution, to function as a responsible adult by collaborating with and helping other people. We heard people talk about how frustrating it is to always be receiving help and about how much they wanted to give something back in the future. The desire to be perceived as a contributing member of society stems from a need to see oneself as independent enough to have an effect upon one's social world. Indeed, the absence of an underlying sense of predictability and autonomy may further undermine our fundamental capacity to see ourselves as part of a wider group, as being social actors rather than isolated observers, as enablers rather than receivers, and as controllers rather than victims.

We believe it is as important to attend to this social dimension as it is to attend to the individual one. To be an autonomous human being means not only to be free to make individual decisions but also to be able to join and act with others for common goals. The twin values of collective responsibility and individual achievement continue to surface in the lives of people apparently deprived of both. The voices of the homeless remind us that they have been robbed not merely of freedom from want or deprivation but also of the freedom to act as responsible and creative adults in a wider social world.

Part of what gives us dignity as human beings is our capacity to be social, to give and take, to love and be loved, to respond and to call forth responses from others. When we speak of treating someone with dignity, we are pointing to our willingness to recognize that person as having feelings, needs, wants, capacities, and the ability to be affected by what we do and how we respond to them. To ignore someone completely, to pretend that person's life is irrelevant or unimportant, undercuts any connection between us and thereby denies that this is a human being who shares in my basic nature. The religious command to see each other as children of God speaks to such an awareness: however we treat each other, the fundamental reality is that we share something that is ultimately more important than all our differences.

The social imperative is as significant as individual autonomy in the creation and upholding of human dignity. People have a right to see themselves, and to be seen, as free agents in appropriate spheres, and limitations on their choice must be justified in terms of protecting their rights or the rights of others. But at the same time, human beings are social beings, depending for their very existence upon other people and thriving only in social settings. Romantic notions of rugged individualism or desert islands aside, human life is based on and in society, and we cannot conceive of a human life without a range of mutual and intertwined relationships with other persons and groups. Only then can we imagine and carry out meaningful life projects.

Because dignity has a social side, people cannot experience themselves as deserving dignity unless they can see themselves within a broader social context. We can make this point genetically, by focusing on the degree of dependence. Human infants are highly dependent on their parents; young children depend on relationships with family and friends to develop a coherent sense of identity; and cultural values and social roles create and reinforce our sense of who we are and what we are capable of doing.

All these types of arguments, however, merely reinforce a moral and religious awareness of the interconnectedness of human beings. We are all more dependent on one another, and on the social institutions we both create and are born into, than we often care to admit. The very concept of human dignity assumes the (admittedly unprovable) assertion of a common life encompassing both rights and responsibilities, individual autonomy and social obligations. To believe that persons are not thoroughly social is to deny any common link, and interaction thus can depend only upon either arbitrary whim or spontaneous emotion. If we believe that human dignity is not merely a descriptive but a normative concept, that we have some obligation to both recognize and respond to its realization in every person, then we must affirm (along with most religious and philosophical traditions) that social solidarity in some form is an essential component of human life, and that its diminishment is a threat not merely to personal happiness but to what it means to be a human being.

It is this sense of shared commonality with other people that is undermined so firmly and devastatingly by the condition of homelessness. On a personal level, homeless persons' daily interactions reveal others to be either indifferent or patronizing. The accounts that homeless parents give in their interviews reveal that, apart from associations with their partners or children, virtually all their other social contacts have been severed. Broader family networks are nonexistent or undependable, often disintegrating in the midst (and because) of the financial and personal problems that led to their homelessness in the first place. Friends and coworkers also have disappeared, either because of the homeless person's solitary social life or because of fear and disillusionment. To lose a job, for example, is to lose not merely a paycheck but an entire social network that helps to bolster one's sense of being a social actor.

The homeless person's remaining social contacts do little to recreate a sense of membership or social solidarity. Most of the people interviewed for our study were single parents, responsible for raising children in a hostile and confusing environment. Family members' mutual dependence, and the need to just get by, undermined the ability of the family to function as anything more than a survival unit. While we did hear some examples of mutual strengthening, most of these people lacked any meaningful adult-to-adult interaction. For those who had partners in the shelters, their relationship was usually severely bruised and battered by the guilt and pain of the preceding months and thus carried too much negative emotional baggage to provide support.

Other homeless people they encounter on the streets or in the shelters tend to elicit fear and distrust more than mutual support or empathy, reminding them of their own marginality and how afraid "the public" is to confront the homeless in our midst face to face. The institutional support people they meet, such as social workers, shelter personnel, hospital emergency room doctors and nurses, and food bank volunteers, are encountered in their role as helpers and providers, thus reinforcing their sense of helplessness and dependence rather than a sense of identification or empowerment.

The structure of their lives, at the same time, prevented any significant sense of solidarity with other people in the shelters. The living conditions isolated them enough to prevent a sense of community from developing, as each family had its own room. And the proximity with other families could be threatening, particularly with the strong socially sanctioned fears of drug abuse, alcoholism, and physical violence. As we saw in chapter 5, many of these families tried to distance themselves as much as possible from the people they lived with in order to avoid contamination or association with a set of problems they wanted to ignore.

To recognize these experiences reminds us how very important individual personal encounters are in recognizing or undermining the dignity of homeless people. It is too easy to conclude that "society" demeans homeless people. When it comes to day-to-day reality, though, what counts is face-to-face contact with individuals, or how many times individuals avoid us. These interpersonal experiences accumulate in the life of a homeless person to communicate a sense of indignity or indifference.

However justified our fear or distrust may be, each time one of us turns away from a person asking for money or refuses to answer a request for aid, we are reinforcing the message that this person is not worthy of my time or attention. Each time a social worker speaks rudely to a homeless person, or when a shelter volunteer fails to acknowledge the fear in a mother's eyes, the social solidarity of this homeless person is further destroyed. We cannot hide behind the anonymity of "society" or "social institutions" in acknowledging the significance of individual encounters in sending messages of who has dignity and who does not.

One of the most debilitating features of the lives of the homeless families in our study is the lack of any stable world or community within which to experience their suffering and confusion. Unlike persecuted communities, these people are going through crisis experiences virtually alone. They are isolated, cut off from all other social support systems that could uphold a self and remind them that they are other than what they are experiencing.

Conclusion

It is one thing to assert philosophically that all persons have dignity; it is quite another to enable people to experience their lives in that way. We have pointed to a set of conditions that seem to be essential if people are to possess that sense of themselves as whole and worthwhile selves: they must have some opportunities for autonomy, predictability, self-expression, and social solidarity with other persons and groups. To undercut these conditions is a serious threat to their dignity.

Homelessness presents a serious and systematic threat to that central need to see oneself as a worthwhile, respectable, and dignified human being. Thinking about the conditions of dignity reminds us how our own lives would be undermined if we lost our homes and how wretched an experience it would be to find ourselves on the street or in a shelter.

8

Dignity and the
Homeless Person

What have we learned about the experiences of homeless families? What conclusions can be drawn from the stories of their lives—and from the ways in which they tell those stories? This concluding chapter provides a few reflections and suggestions about what these experiences tell us about our society, our values, and our own lives.

First, on the basis of our having been immersed for two years in the stories and experiences of homeless families, we believe it is virtually impossible to adopt a neutral or purely objective tone in discussing this problem. We do not apologize for this inability; we merely report it. As observers, however, we can still be honest and fair in sorting out what we have heard. Throughout this book we have tried to allow the stories to suggest differing interpretations, including some that are not altogether praiseworthy. We have resisted the temptation to assume that everything people say must be taken at face value or that these families are simply helpless victims of an evil social system.

But it is equally important to try to feel what their experiences are like and to acknowledge that there is something very wrong with a wealthy country that continues to tolerate such experiences. This point was made very effectively by two members of the Institute of Medicine Committee who attacked the refusal of the institute to publish a supplementary statement to its report on homelessness. In a letter supporting the statement, they wrote: "As a matter of intellectual integrity, we believe that homelessness cannot be discussed without conveying a tone of shame and outrage, without attention to systemic causes, and without reference to public policy and political decisions, which invariably entail political actions."[1]

Causes and Response

In the first chapter we suggested that there are two different approaches to understanding the causes of homelessness. On the one hand, it is possible to assume an individualistic perspective that examines factors within a homeless person's life history and decision-making that predispose them to becoming homeless. From an individualistic vantagepoint one can usually identify one or two precipitating factors that result in a family becoming homeless, such as the breakup of a relationship or poor financial judgment. Individualistic explanations are often more psychological in probing family history experiences, such as childhood sexual abuse, that seem to correlate with homelessness.

In contrast, structural explanations tend to explain homelessness in terms of high unemployment rates, lack of available low-income housing, a low minimum wage, and welfare payments that are intended to punish their recipients. Structural explanations hold society accountable for homelessness and emphasize changes in government policy. In contrast, individualistic theories of homelessness commonly take one of two approaches: either they focus on rehabilitating homeless people through psychological counseling and intervention, or else they draw the conclusion that homeless people simply must learn to be more responsible and take charge of their own lives.

Liberals have typically preferred structural theories that suggest greater government intervention in the lives of poor people. In contrast, conservatives tend to place the emphasis on individual accountability. A cross-cutting variable, however, is whether one conceives of intervention being fundamentally a psychological or sociological task. Psychologists and psychiatrists, for example, have tended to emphasize individual and group therapy as a way of solving past problems (such as sexual abuse), whereas those with a more sociological orientation often stress the importance of creating social support networks that connect an individual to social institutions (including family networks) within the community.

We recognize the human tendency to simplify explanations of the world, especially morally troubling problems such as the existence of homeless families. But we refuse to side with either an individualistic or a structural explanation of homelessness. Society has a responsibility to assist its least fortunate members. Nevertheless, to place the responsibility for homelessness exclusively on the shoulders of legislators is to remove any responsibility from homeless persons to take charge of their lives.

When the blame for homelessness is placed on society, the implication is that homeless persons are societal victims. Then the responsibility for solving homelessness is that of legislators who make policy. From this perspective, homelessness is a problem to be solved, and the moral agency of the homeless person is too often discounted. On the other hand, when a purely individualistic approach is taken, homeless people are blamed for their situation and the bond that connects the citizens of a society into a community of mutual responsibility is lost. Instead, the prevailing view of society becomes one of possessive individualism, where each person watches out for his or her own interests.

In this book we have tried to skirt the causal issues, in part because the data from the interviews revealed the enormous complexity of reasons for which people become homeless and the ways in which individual and social factors are closely intertwined. We are convinced that the more individualistic approaches err in ascribing too much responsibility (or even blame) to the people who are homeless, forgetting that it is not accidental that certain types of people tend to become incapacitated in certain ways. Similarly, the more social approaches often go astray in ignoring (or at least downplaying) the ways in which individuals do in fact make poor decisions about their lives, and the extent to which even the poorest among us continue to be responsible in some ways for their lives and their futures. We hope that it is possible to recognize individual responsibility when it exists without thereby blaming the victim for being homeless.

We admit that when we began our study, we were more predisposed toward the social explanations. Although we continue to recognize the centrality of such factors as the lack of affordable housing, listening to the respondents has forced us to appreciate more fully the personal and individualized features of their decisions, actions, and life-styles.

Indeed, the very fact that our sample of homeless families is skewed in the direction of the most healthy and well-adjusted homeless people makes this finding even more noteworthy. As noted earlier, the five shelters that housed the families are among the very best in Los Angeles, and most are quite selective in screening out people with severe personal problems such as drug abuse or mental illness. It is therefore striking that virtually all the respondents presented accounts that involved both systemic and individual behavioral causes for their homelessness. As we have seen, their stories abound with instances of drug and alcohol addiction, physical and sexual abuse, unstable personal relationships, and poor coping and decision-making skills.

Recognizing the complexity of the causes of homelessness leads to a more realistic awareness of the danger of attributing causes at all. The most immediate causal answer is usually a purely financial one: a person is homeless because of the inability to pay for a place to live. If society provided a free abode for every citizen, there would be little or no homelessness. But to ask why some people become homeless, while others do not, immerses us in the rich and confusing world of individual family stories, a world within which we have attempted to stay throughout the course of this book.

It should also be noted that there are often ideological reasons for focusing on causation. If we can identify individual decisions or attributes as key reasons, we are more likely to be able either to blame the people or seek out public or private assistance to "cure" the individual problems. Similarly, believing that broader social ills are the "real" cause allows us to focus on large-scale public commitments to provide more housing and educational and employment opportunities. Although we are convinced that such solutions would be helpful, it is simply misleading to pretend that any one or two individual- or social-level changes would "solve" the problem of family homelessness.

The search for causation is less helpful than the question of how to *respond* to people who are homeless. The underlying moral reality is that these families are homeless, that they are in need, and that there are various types of resources to help them. Although causal language certainly cannot be avoided entirely, it has tended to distract attention from present needs to past history. People are homeless right now because they have no place to live and cannot afford to live anywhere else. It is *this* reality that calls for a response, both from individuals and from society.

Homelessness is an assault on the dignity of persons, and most especially on the dignity of homeless parents and their children. Deep within the human spirit is a tendency to blame others. Hence, even among advocates for the homeless there is a pervasive attitude regarding the "worthy homeless"—those who are homeless because of circumstances beyond their control. We resist such categorizations. Persons are worthy of respect, even if their actions and life-styles are not praiseworthy.

There is another reason to avoid simple social-level causal explanations. We have insisted on approaching these people in terms of the category of dignity; we prefer to view them as responsible adults rather than assuming from the outset that they are all helpless victims who can only respond passively to their environments. And, indeed, we have seen in their interviews how frequently they view themselves in active terms, how often they see their own complicity in their situation. If we are to continue to learn how to recognize and honor their capacities as moral agents, adopting a perspective tending to empower rather than undermine them, then we are forced to take them seriously as actors in their own dramas. Such a perspective makes us more likely to recognize the varying degrees of responsibility they have for what has happened to them. We can thus attempt to avoid both extreme reactions of patronizing or blaming them: we will not reject or dismiss them as irresponsible people, but neither can we assume that they simply need to be sheltered by a more enlightened and powerful government, social agency, or individual.

At the same time, we cannot minimize the social problems associated with poverty. We are not attempting to judge these families, nor can we, as observers, fully understand the nature of the choices they have made. We agree fully with both the content and the tone of Jonathan Kozol's powerful statement on Americans' reactions to homeless families:

> We do not know what we ought to do about an underclass. We do know that we should not manufacture one. We do not know how to bring an end to poverty and inequality in our society. We do know children shouldn't live in subways. We also have a good idea of how to build a house—or many houses, each of which has many heated, safe, well-lighted rooms, doors with doorknobs, electric switches that go on and off, a stove that can be used to cook nutritious meals, a refrigerator in which food for children can be stored. Overwhelmed by knowledge of the things we can't do, we are also horrified that we do not do what we can. I suspect that one of the ways we deal with this is to get angry—not at ourselves, but at the mother and, by implication, at the child.[2]

In short, we must try to recognize that homeless families are part of a world quite familiar to all of us—a world in which what happens is a combination of our own personal choices and resources along with the many factors of chance and social factors that are out of our control. The interviews, and the attention we have tried to pay to listening to the experiences of homeless families as they themselves described them, allow us to identify with their situations precisely because we see ourselves in them—that they, like us, are human beings who have tried to act and make decisions in the midst of a complex web of social interactions and pressures.

We will not be able to identify with them at all, however, if we begin by assuming that they are powerless children or helpless victims caught up in processes over which they have absolutely no control. Being homeless does not deprive people of their capacity to act, and these families remind us of the ways in which all of us are inevitably both acting and acted upon in our daily lives. To ignore either of these poles of human life is to deny the very essence of these people's struggle, and it undermines our capacity to view them as deserving of the dignity that is so vital to their acceptance and help.

Our decision to hold these two poles together and our decision to refrain from finding a causal explanation for why these families are homeless stem from our desire to acknowledge the dignity they continue to deserve.

Homelessness and Poverty

One important conclusion that must be drawn from this awareness is that any efforts to ameliorate the homeless problem must begin by addressing the larger and more fundamental problem of poverty, particularly by recognizing the extent to which so many poor people are in danger of becoming homeless. However much shelters and other homeless-related programs are needed, we cannot pretend that they are anything other than temporary expedients that do nothing to deal with the reasons why people are homeless.

We must remember the fact that, as the Institute of Medicine study insisted, "Shelters were not originally intended to be broad-based human service systems and are poorly designed to serve that purpose."[3] This is an extremely important point, as it redirects our attention to the broader problem of homelessness and prevents us from expecting the shelter system to solve them. While more services should be considered where feasible, it is simply a fact of life that shelters, by their very nature, are ill-equipped to deal with the housing market or with the various abuse problems (alcohol, drug, and physical) of so many homeless families.

Sadly, we must conclude that the same thing must be said about the need for more affordable housing. This is not to say that such housing should not be built; indeed, listening to the stories of the homeless should convince us of the central importance of having a place to live, and anything that can be done to improve the availability and affordability of housing should be done. But if we are honest with ourselves in listening to these stories, we have to recognize that housing problems are often the symptoms, or the results, of a set of deeper and more endemic difficulties.

Ellen Bassuk has emphasized the multidimensional nature of the problem and the way in which proposed solutions must address the long-term and more endemic personal issues of the homeless population: "Our major goal should be to rescue these families, particularly the children, from a lifetime of deprivation and violence and to interfere with a newly emergent cycle of intergenerational homelessness. Without long-term solutions that focus on both the seriousness of the housing crisis and the emotional problems of the mothers and children, the plight of these families will continue to be desperate."[4]

From the standpoint of social policy, perhaps the most powerful lesson we can learn from the voices of homeless families is that we are in the process of creating a generation of people who are homeless both literally and figuratively. The stories lived out by so many of these women—replete with repeated accounts of failed relationships, physical and emotional abuse, incoherent careers, and unforeseen tragedies—remind us of how hard it is to climb out of poverty and dead ends. The personal adult tragedies are merely compounded when we look at the lives of their children and realize the conditions in which they live and the difficulties *they* will have in turn. The interlocking nature of the social problems behind homelessness for these families makes it extremely difficult to devise social policies to address the problem; but it also makes such policies more essential, if only to try to avoid the endless continuation of the cycle.

What sorts of policy recommendations would flow from such an awareness? Our data do not enable us to add very much to the suggestions that regularly appear in the many books and articles on the subject. But we would call particular attention to several related issues based on recurrent themes in the interviews.

First, it is clear that there is little point in perpetuating a financial social support system that gives families barely enough money or opportunity to climb out of their situation. While we recognize the financial limitations of a government facing massive deficits and rising social needs, it is important to recognize the points where the system's failings can only be remedied by the infusion of more money.

For example, whether or not the minimum wage is increased, attention must be paid to the underlying issue of those often lumped together as "the working poor." Women told us that they would love to work, but that their salary would provide little more than day care for their children and a very flimsy roof over their heads. Most of the respondents could only hold down entry-level positions in occupations requiring little or no specialized skills. As long as such jobs do not provide enough money to support a family, there is little point in urging people to look for permanent work.

In addition, the interviews suggest that available and safe child care would make an enormous difference in the lives of these people. The single mother with several children is in the most difficult and precarious position, and only child care is likely to free her from a life of drifting from shelter to shelter. The homeless mothers in our study are adamant about how trapped they feel, and how finding a productive and permanent job seems out of reach as long as they have young children.

Not only does the welfare system fail to provide enough help, it actually offers disincentives for people to reattain some sense of personal dignity and empowerment. For example, must we accept the frequent insensitivity and poor training of welfare workers as inevitable? If welfare mothers were viewed as an important voting constituency, they would not be victimized by their providers as often as they are today.

But the welfare system is merely representative of the deeper way in which our attempted solutions so often become the source of new problems. To blame the insensitive welfare worker is to blame ourselves. Indeed, the worker may have more reasons for insensitivity, considering the working conditions and the all-too-human need to cushion oneself from painful and traumatic experiences.[5]

Peter Marin has written powerfully about the ways in which "our supposed sources of support . . . have caused the problem in the first place." He explains the refusal of many people to accept the offer of help as "a mute, furious refusal, a self-imposed exile" that reflects our inability to provide any relief to the sense of isolation of so many of our fellow citizens. Instead of gratefully accepting our offers of help and shelter, "they are clinging to their freedom and their space, and they do not believe that this is what we, with our inadequate and grudging programs and shelters, mean to allow them."[6] Similar points have been made about many elements of the institutional structures that undercut dignity in their often well-meaning efforts to respond to homelessness. Our social programs tend to establish unreasonable criteria for eligibility, prohibit money from being used for special purposes that a person might deem more important and crucial, and mandate waiting periods that leave people unable to either cope with or predict what is going to happen next.[7]

The decisions we make creating and designing shelters can also take into account the dignity concerns of homeless families. For example, more attention must be paid to "softer" concerns such as autonomy and privacy in developing shelter rules and organizing facilities. The symbolism of small factors, such as having a place where people can make telephone calls without being overheard, should not be overlooked.

Indeed, just as our society increasingly requires environmental impact statements before new structures or physical developments are erected, perhaps we should consider applying the types of human dignity criteria we have discussed to social policies concerning the homeless. A "dignity impact statement" might force us to recognize the more intangible effects of social policy decisions on those affected by them. For example, our legislators should ask what are the effects of particular proposals and social systems upon the capacity of homeless families to regain some control over their own lives, upon their ability to see the world as predictable and dependable, and upon their ability to be treated as functioning and valuable members of American society. Policies that infantilize, policies that confuse, and policies that isolate are all to be avoided, not merely for economic or political reasons, but for moral reasons as well.

Ambivalences in American Views of Dignity

Whether we refer to individual discomfort or broad social policies, the difficulties experienced by American society in responding to homeless people reflect some deeper confusions at the level of basic values. Societies are defined, in large part, precisely by the mixture of values and beliefs that both form its citizens and are in turn formed by them. If we wonder why we are willing to tolerate the continuing plight of homeless people or why we are torn between compassion for them and distancing ourselves from them, our search should include considering these underlying commitments and confusions, which define us as Americans. By identifying some of these value polarities we can begin to clarify the rather different responses that are currently made to the presence of homeless persons on our streets.[8]

First, recall the tension between an individual versus a social understanding of dignity. Is our dignity an *individual* attribute, to be appealed to vis-á-vis other individuals? Or is dignity a *shared* characteristic of human beings in society, to be recognized and mutually reinforced? This tension becomes apparent in the attempts to derive specific human rights from the notion of dignity, particularly when these rights involve socially provided resources such as shelter, food, or health care. In the individualistic emphasis, it is my personal dignity which is at stake, and society is responsible for protecting or ensuring that my dignity is respected. In the more social emphasis, the community as a whole carries the dignity as a human society, and attention is likely to be directed more toward individual responsibilities than individual claims. This tension is lived out in arguments concerning the lives of homeless families, particularly in terms of concern for the right to shelter.

This ambivalence simply reflects the age-old tension between communalism and individualism in American society. A wide range of writers have decried the extreme individualism that seems to have pervaded our history, and which often is viewed as defining the American character.[9] But it is easy to overemphasize one side of this pole and to forget that much of the early success of American life was based on a much more communitarian ethic, one that remains an important force in American society. It is being rediscovered both in many communities and in management theories developed in response to the decline of American industrial strength.[10]

In their recent work, Robert Bellah and his coauthors point out the pivotal conflict between the American values of autonomy and sociality. In the following passage, notice the way in which the conflict is both built into the very nature of our culture and at the same time is unable to be resolved without sacrificing either value:

> The inner tensions of American individualism add up to a classic case of ambivalence. We strongly assert the value of our self-reliance and autonomy. We deeply feel the emptiness of a life without sustaining social commitments. Yet we are hesitant to articulate our sense that we need one another as much as we need to stand alone, for fear that if we did we would lose our independence altogether. The tensions of our lives would be even greater if we did not, in fact, engage in practices that constantly limit the effects of an isolating individualism, even though we cannot articulate those practices nearly as well as we can the quest for autonomy.[11]

This insight applies even more starkly to our homeless families, precisely because they have experienced the costs of losing (or, in some cases, never having) the social connections and support that may have saved them from their present situation.

Second, there is a fundamental tension in American society between *competition* and *cooperation*. Do we ultimately judge ourselves (as individuals and as a society) in terms of relative standing or in terms of shared attainments or living conditions? This tension is a fundamental ambivalence, built into the very structure of our lives; we receive mixed messages from the time we are born in virtually every arena of life. Doing well in school is competitive, when grades are assigned, tests are standardized, and admission is selective. But getting along with others is also prized, and our teachers are often caught on the horns of an uncomfortable dilemma: how can they reward an individual's hard work without sending the message that the reward signifies the ultimate value of competition? Whether or not there is a gender basis for this particular value tension (as has been suggested in some recent literature), Americans are likely to have trouble deciding between competitive and cooperative orientations.

This ambivalence is significant in the way we view people who find themselves deprived of economic or political resources. How many of us secretly compare ourselves to those "below" us? Are we not, at some level, reassured by the fact that our lives could indeed be much worse? However strong the incentive to help those less fortunate, there remains the uncomfortable thought that sharing may mean losing, that pulling someone up may risk pulling myself down, and that, since there will always be winners and losers, I would prefer to be a winner. However much we believe that our true heroes are those who serve, it is hard not to hear the alternative messages sent in terms of salaries, benefits, and power perquisites heaped on the most competitive among us.

Third, American society continues to struggle with the tension between *achieved* and *ascribed* status. Is our basic worth defined by what we do and accomplish, or is it defined simply by who we are? In the sociological literature, ascribed characteristics usually refer to determined features such as race or sex, but we can easily understand "humanity" as an ascribed characteristic as well. To raise the question challenges our very sense of self-worth: who among us is not convinced that success (however defined) somehow adds to our value or worth, or that we have a right to be treated differently if we have accomplished more?

The ambivalence is strongest in the area of our assessment of accomplishment versus ascription as the basis for social values. But however important this distinction between achievement and intrinsic worth may be, too much can be made of it. In much of the current conservative backlash against liberal concepts of welfare and rights, for example, there is the suggestion that one chooses either to value achievement or to value people for some other reason. The traditional recognition and admiration of accomplishment can exist side by side with a deeper acknowledgment of a dignity owed to all persons. In recognizing our tendency to be pulled in both directions, we need not deny either side.[12]

When we are faced with evaluating personal worth, this tension is often expressed in terms of the values of *activity* versus *passivity*. We suspect that our readers would readily agree that Americans are obsessed with action, that the pace of most of our lives leaves little room for the value of being rather than doing, and that most of us are likely to feel guilty doing nothing. The achievement orientation compels us to attend to what we do; it is difficult to be willing to wait, to relax, to attend to what is happening, to be patient. But the very awareness of this tendency is evidence of the (perhaps growing) alternative value, and of the ways in which we are being called to question the extent to which activity is emphasized.

The valuing of activity makes it extremely difficult to respond in a neutral fashion to the lives of homeless people. One problem is that, from our standards, they often appear to be doing nothing: they may not work, or send their children to schools, or create anything tangible. Adopting a narrow definition of activity, it is all too easy for us to move to a judgmental position, or at least to feel that their lives are somehow incomplete or worthless because they are not being active. We might suggest that our tendency to judge them in this way stems from the fact that we judge ourselves in the same way; the problem lies not in others but in ourselves.[13]

One aspect of this tension, which is particularly relevant for our purposes, is our polity's ambivalent view toward property. Most of us, we suspect, are willing to make a value distinction between personal rights and property rights; perhaps the appeal to the latter by segregationists in the 1950s and 1960s has given property rights a bad name. In the abstract, we seem to have moved (in both constitutional interpretation and everyday life) to a position that gives more priority to nonproperty features of life.

But the issue is not so clear when the discussion moves from the abstract to the particular. Acknowledging the secondary role of property is more difficult if I am being asked to give up something I own or something I have built. In one important strand of the liberal political tradition, of course, property is defined as an extension of the self, as something of myself that has been mixed in with the physical world and therefore remains "mine" in some important sense. One need not be a Lockean or a Marxist to recognize the power of such analogies; however, we must acknowledge that the choices between my "property" and your "human needs" are difficult ones indeed. As hard as it is to admit, if we were truly committed to the secondary importance of property rights, we might feel compelled to give away most of what we own in order to help feed and clothe other people.

Still another important value tension that affects our understanding of and response to homelessness is what Talcott Parsons referred to as *"affectivity"* versus *"neutrality."*[14] For our purposes, what is important in this tension is the extent to which each of us feels compelled to respond to social problems in both impassioned and dispassionate terms. We are put off by the purely academic, aloof tone of those who treat homeless people as simply one more social issue to be examined and dissected. But we also are likely to be repelled by those advocates who seem to be so committed to one side or the other that they are unable to gain any removed perspective or to allow themselves (or anyone else) to sort out the issues in a more objective manner. As a result, we find ourselves either bouncing back and forth between extreme concern and utter objectivity or else trying to find some compromise position of cautious concern or engaged analysis.

We might note that it is not merely the observers who are caught in this ambivalence. In their interviews, homeless people themselves struggle with this same problem. Should they try to adopt a more removed view of their own lives, trying to explain to the researcher how they came to be homeless and sort out the factors responsible for landing them in the shelter? Or should they use the interview as an opportunity to vent their frustration and anger, to seek help or comfort or understanding, or to draw the interviewer into their own experiences? We are not surprised that they have the same tensions, because both engagement and objectivity are highly valued in the society in which we all live.

Finally, we would mention the tension between a *particularistic* and a *universalistic* approach to community. In the American context, this ambivalence is lived out in terms of whether we experience homeless families as part of our social world in anything other than a purely formal sense. In other words, do we have any obligations toward them? Are we tied (morally, emotionally, politically) to them? It may not be enough to acknowledge that they are fellow citizens. Are they also members of our community, with shared obligations and responsibilities?

Answering this question is so difficult because, once again, we hear conflicting emphases from the larger society. We are proud of communities whose members "stick together," "take care of their own," and provide for each other. But most of our models refer either to small localities or to ethnic or religious subgroups, leaving open the question of the connection with the wider society. If taking care of one's own means giving priority to those closest or more familiar or more similar, what happens to those who are on the outside? The value tension appears when we recognize the heroism of people who in fact move outside of established boundaries and are able to redefine their obligations in a more global sense.

Religious traditions provide little help here, precisely because they are caught in the same ambivalence. For the mainstreams of both Judaism and Christianity, we recognize the difficulty of applying the ethical norms of love of neighbor or of shared responsibility. The question, Who is my neighbor?

remains one of the most difficult issues in religious ethics. To what extent are we obligated to care for everyone equally, in a world where most of us have specific relationships with individuals and groups that appear to make particular claims upon us?

This ambivalence makes us most uncomfortable when we recognize the trade-offs we are constantly forced to make between our special relationships and our wider universalistic obligations. If we were talking about the same level of needs, the dilemma might be more easily resolved. After all, I might justify providing food for my family rather than for someone I don't know because I love my family and I know that I can't feed everyone. But the truly troubling choices (of which we manage to remain unaware most of the time) involve choosing between an extra car for my family or a year's worth of food for someone else, or between a larger house for myself and some minimal shelter for several strangers. Once again, we are not provided with very clear guidance from societal values in making our decisions; as a result, we may retreat to a stance of ignoring the wider needs or resenting the claims themselves as intruding on our own choices.

To summarize, this discussion, however brief and general, has identified some of the key value tensions within our wider society. Our often ambivalent and ill-defined responses to homeless people stem from these value conflicts and reveal the continued strength of these conflicts in our daily lives. As we have suggested, homeless families, as members of the same society, share these ambivalent values as well. Indeed, it may be harder for them to live in the tension because so much of their own self-worth is at stake.

Cultural Lessons of Homelessness

What do the experiences of homeless people, and our responses to those experiences, teach us about American society in the early 1990s? The most important lesson may be simply that such experiences are allowed to exist. At the level of moral sensitivity, all of us should be struck by the commonplace but powerful recognition of the depth and variety of poverty and economic despair that exist in the midst of the wealth and opportunity of the United States. Simply to acknowledge that fact is to take an important step toward the discomfort and shame that precedes any movement into social action or individual response.

In addition, when we reflect on our discussion of the ambivalent values concerning dignity in our society, the voices of these homeless families compel us to face the reality of both sides of those values that define us as distinctively American. In spite of its homespun appeal, it simply will not do to insist that people can "pull themselves up by their bootstraps" in the age-old American tradition; but neither is it plausible to conclude that all assertions of personal responsibility are tantamount to blaming the victim. If we listen to the stories, and to the interpretations that intrude themselves on both the homeless people and on us, we are more likely to be struck by the enormous complexity of human life in a society that cherishes both responsibility and dependence, both individual rights and social solidarity.

Instead of seeking a more clear-cut value system in American culture, or simply choosing one side of the tension as more essential or fundamental, we suggest that the core obligation is to struggle (both as individuals and as a society) to avoid the paralysis that is likely to result from these ambivalences. The people we admire—those who are able to take a stand, to devote part of their lives to a more selfless pursuit of social justice—are not necessarily people who feel any less ambivalently than we do. They are likely to be people who have felt called to act within the ambivalence, to push forward in one direction of response to need.

In fact, a somewhat optimistic interpretation would suggest that this very capacity to respond in the midst of ambivalence is itself one important feature of "the American character." To be able to act in the midst of uncertainty, to begin anew with few guarantees, has enabled people to move west, invent social systems and technology, and struggle for new values in ways that continue to impress us. One need not adopt a chauvinistic or "America First" mentality to recognize the deep-seated value of responding to ambivalence by acting in the face of uncertainty.

This capacity to act is both our greatest social opportunity and our greatest social sin. The opportunity exists to continue to respond to the poor and the homeless, not as outsiders but as fellow citizens. We can reaffirm with them our common commitment to build something better, to view American society as something more than simply an assortment of diverse people. The image of seeing the United States as "the city on the hill" remains strong in many of us, and it should not be dismissed simply as patriotic posturing or religious fanaticism.

But the very same values are largely responsible for the insensitivity to poverty in our society. We become so fixated on the need to act, to change, to "do," that values such as dignity and acceptance and tolerance are submerged. To define ourselves in terms of our work or our accomplishments leads inexorably to diminishing those who can not easily find work or point to accomplishments of their own. To believe that anything is possible creates unrealistic expectations that, when applied to people whose lives are mired in disappointment and tragedy, can only result in disdain and distancing.

The experiences of the homeless families in this book can remind us not only of the meaning and depth of these values but also of their dangers and distractions. We would suggest that underlying the disappointment and occasional bitterness in their voices is a more fundamental sense of frustration with the very values by which they (like us) are so defined. If these people were convinced that they really were helpless, they would not be so depressed by their inability to care for their children; if they were convinced that work was not important, they would not be so desperate to find meaningful work. If we listen carefully, we hear the same tensions that motivate our own discomfort and ambivalent attitudes in confronting them and their life situations.

And this is precisely what we must expect, if we remember that they are part of our society. Even the recent immigrant is infused with a whole set of expectations, simply by virtue of living in this society. Indeed, it can be argued that the selection process makes it more likely that most people who come to this country are already "like us" in some very important ways.[15] Their disappointment in not living up to our cultural values simply mirrors our disappointment that *we* have not lived up to them as well.

As part of what we usually consider to be the most vulnerable segment of our society, these homeless families (especially single women with young children) provide an important test of where our values are incarnated in the social world. How we treat them—as people often devoid of meaningful jobs, income, social status, or even identifiable talents or future possibilities—tells us something about our lived-out commitment to human dignity. In teaching us about where our commitments really lie, in not allowing us to avert our gaze or our concern, these families can help redirect us to the enacted values that allow them to continue to live as they do. They can force us to rethink our own responses to the ways in which these tensions are experienced by so many of our fellow citizens.

To sum up, let us turn once again to the obvious ways in which the experiences of the homeless recounted in this book involved threats to their personal dignity. Oscar Schachter has identified specific forms of conduct that are "antithetical or incompatible with respect for inherent dignity." He specifies the following forms (among others):

—Statements that demean and humiliate individuals or groups because of their origins, *status* or beliefs. . . .
—Denial of the capacity of a person to assert claims to basic rights. . . .
—Dissemination of negative stereotypes of groups (ethnic, religious, *social*) and implications that members of such groups are inferior. . . .
—Degrading living conditions and deprivation of basic needs. . . .
—Abuse and insolence by officials, especially to persons suffering from infirmities or *social opprobrium*.[16]

Whether or not the reader agrees that all these forms of action are violations of clear human rights, it is hard not to recognize the experiences in our accounts in this discussion written ten years ago without any reference to either American society or the situation of homeless families.

Individual Responses to the Homeless

The quest for dignity is, in many respects, the quest for the conditions of a responsible adult life. The interviews have uncovered a range of such conditions and have revealed both the ways in which homelessness threatens dignity and the extent to which people will go to recreate some sense of dignity for themselves and their families.

But what of our own responsibility as persons who are not homeless but who are fellow citizens of those who are? It is too easy to redefine homelessness as a broad social policy problem and to see its solution solely in long-term political change. Until the day when homeless people are provided with adequate opportunities to escape from their current situation, the individual questions remain, whether in face-to-face confrontations on the streets or in other requests for assistance.[17]

In our earlier discussion, we have identified the importance of specific episodes in the lives of the people we have spoken with. For the homeless person, "the welfare system" is not so much an abstract entity but a succession of specific individuals and groups who respond to them in very concrete ways. Similarly, society's reaction to homelessness does not consist simply of broad public policy choices; it is made up of all the interactions and avoidances experienced by the homeless person every day.

Therefore, we need to remember that our own individualized reactions are part of the way American society responds to homelessness. In crossing the street to avoid a homeless person, we are helping to create a definition of that person's isolation; in giving money to someone in a subway, we are fostering a type of connection. We chose not to generalize about whether such responses are right or wrong. What is crucial, we believe, is to acknowledge the extent to which our own personal choices are fundamental answers to the question of how American society deals with people who are homeless.

In the light of this awareness, we must attend very carefully to stereotyping the homeless and recognize that the depth of this problem is revealed most strikingly in the extent to which they themselves engage in such attitudes. We have documented the ways in which so many of the homeless adults in our study distance themselves from other people in their situation and the ways in which they often adopt the same brutalizing and superficial responses others use to deny them assistance or support.

It is apparent that the societal attitude toward the homeless has never been very positive, but it appears to be getting worse. We would surmise (although we hope we are wrong) that public concern over the homeless issue may be cresting and may be about to be replaced by a growing backlash. Social commentators have referred to "compassion fatigue" as being one of the hallmarks of the 1990s, and debates about the federal deficit and taxes are liable to only exacerbate these feelings.

Los Angeles itself provides some cautionary warnings in this regard. In April 1989 Proposition 3 was defeated in a public referendum. This proposal would have provided city bonds of $100 million to help renovate three to nine thousand low-rent apartments. Although 64.7 percent of the voters supported it, it failed to attain the requisite two-thirds vote. What is particularly significant is that Proposition 3 was the "lowest funded and least publicized" of four bond measures on the same ballot, and the other three passed easily. Most observers cited lack of an organized housing movement as the key reason for its failure.[18]

Several months later a *Los Angeles Times* article cited the following examples of hardening attitudes toward the homeless:

> West Hollywood, one of the cities most receptive to the homeless, is cutting by more than half the number of people it will house in an auditorium on cold nights. The city is also moving a free-meal program out of Plummer Park.

> Santa Monica, another bastion of tolerance toward the homeless, is reducing by one hundred the number of people it will feed in its popular Ocean Park feeding program. Local businessmen there have complained that street people are driving customers away.

> Trailers purchased by Los Angeles as transitional housing for homeless families have been vandalized in Harbor City and Pacoima.[19]

Many of the negative attitudes were summarized by the president of the Santa Monica Chamber of Commerce, who is quoted as saying: "I think it's called 'limits of tolerance.' It's just becoming overwhelming. Aggressive panhandling, defecating and urinating in business doorways, scaring customers with drunk and lewd behavior—these are the things we can't tolerate any more."[20]

If there is a developing backlash, it is certainly understandable. People become tired and impatient hearing about the same issue over and over again, particularly when no progress seems to be made. How many documentaries or books are we willing to be bombarded with before we say, "Enough is enough"? The direct contact most Americans have with homeless people is likely to embarrass or frustrate them. Our daily urban confrontations with the homeless usually leave us wishing they (and the entire problem they represent) would just go away and leave us alone.

But such reactions, however predictable, cannot be our last word on the subject. People remain in need, and we must not simply put them out of our minds. As individuals, we should try to ask ourselves why they make us so uncomfortable, without drawing the conclusion that our discomfort destroys our obligation.

It is clear that our responses to homeless people reflect the preconceptions we bring to their situation. In a fascinating summary of the history of American homelessness, Charles Hoch uncovered four periods in which different images of the homeless were prevalent. In the late eighteenth and early nineteenth centuries, the homeless person was the "vagrant," a wandering person who chose to be in that condition because he could not fit in with society. After the Civil War this image was replaced by that of the "tramp," the down-and-out person who had lost everything and had chosen to respond by riding the rails or wandering the streets. In the early twentieth century the homeless person was seen as a "deviant," suffering from some internal psychological or emotional problems outside of his control. And more recently we have focused on the image of the "victim," the person suffering from social and systemic injustice or inequality who cannot respond in any other way.

Hoch correctly points out the different ways in which each of us tend to view such images and how important they are in defining the options available to us to respond to the homeless:

> Missionaries devoted to converting the immoral and police committed to incarcerating the unlawful tend to perceive the homeless as vagrants or tramps whose predicament is self-imposed. In contrast, psychiatrists and psychologists focus on the causes of individual mental and physiological illness that set the homeless apart as deviant or disabled, while social workers and organizers tend to explore how institutional forces have pushed people out of their shelter.[21]

We are likely to be affected by the way homeless people act toward us or by the attitudes they seem to adopt toward the help we offer them. But our perception of their actions is colored by these images we bring with us. If we begin with the assumption that they are essentially victims, we will be more willing to overlook their demands or their appearance than if we begin by viewing them as vagrants or tramps. Are we willing or able to understand that many behaviors that we would never tolerate in our friends or acquaintances may be survival mechanisms adopted by people who are desperate, isolated, and threatened? Similarly, whether we are able to empathize with them is influenced by whether we begin by labeling them as deviant, and therefore "not like us."

We have seen the difficulty of defining homeless people in a one-dimensional way, and we should therefore recognize that no single image is ever able to do justice to the full range of causes and experiences. However, in the interests of pointing toward a renewed way to take their lives seriously, and to hold together the perspectives we have heard, we suggest the image of "pilgrim" as a particularly appropriate one for our time.

This image is a rich one, embedded deeply in the American consciousness. In this word, we are reminded of a group of early European immigrants, escaping one society for a new and yet uncharted one. This sense of escape mixed with hope, when applied to homeless families, underscores both their past and present suffering and their hopes for a future that will allow them to build something else.

In a more general sense, pilgrims are people in transition, without a stable residence or place to really call their own. We often speak of them as being "in, but not of" the world they inhabit, people marginalized both in space and time. What image could more accurately capture the experience of a homeless family, outcasts from a stable existence forced to continue to survive in a world to which they do not fully belong?

The concept of being a pilgrim has deep religious roots, of course. As we suggested earlier, we think of the ways in which both Judaism and Christianity command respect and caring for the sojourner and the wayfarer. And both traditions (as well as Islam) have an image of human life as a pilgrimage from birth to death. We are to see ourselves as inhabitants of another realm, of another dimension, as we move through this tangible and created world. However much we value or cherish our current lives and our earth, these religious traditions remind us, it is not only the outwardly "homeless" whose lives are rooted somewhere else.

Finally, the image of the pilgrim may allow us to acknowledge and affirm both the passive and the active dimensions of homeless families. Pilgrims are affected by their surroundings; they are indeed victims of intolerance, of oppression, of meaninglessness. But, as pilgrims, they are also actors, putting one foot ahead of the other, responsible for what happens next and for responding to what has happened before. To view the homeless person as a pilgrim may allow the rest of us to escape from the twin perils of either blaming them or absolving them of all responsibility. All of us are caught in webs not of our own making, but we must acknowledge our roles and get on with our lives; similarly, homeless families can be viewed and responded to as people struggling from one hard place to a potentially better life, without assuming that they are either saints or demons.

To view homeless families as pilgrims is to remind ourselves of our own status as pilgrims as well, and to share with them a common human experience of living in a world that, for all its splendor and hope and possibility, still falls short of offering us heaven. It is the struggle to move our lives and our society a little closer to that vision that defines us as human beings with the dignity linked to being created in a divine image.

Motivation and Responsibility

Guilt is sometimes a good motivator, but it is also a complex one. We suspect most of us feel some twinge of guilt in seeing an increasing number of people standing at highway intersections holding signs that read, "I will work for food." Does this guilt push us to think about their situation, to respond in some way to meet their need (whether this involves giving them money, searching out a shelter to do volunteer work, or working for legislation to provide more affordable housing)? Or does it make us angry and resentful, leading us to push them out of our minds or to walk around convincing ourselves that they, not we, are really to blame?

As we were completing the manuscript for this book, Mitch Snyder committed suicide in his shelter in Washington, D.C. Snyder was probably the best known national advocate for the homeless, and his many public fasts and mass actions had spurred the city and federal government to provide more assistance. Snyder's major tactic was to force people to confront their own responsibility for the situation, and he often did so by applying public pressure in ways that were often interpreted as blackmail.

In reflecting on his efforts, we are led to ask ourselves, What events would motivate *us* to act? There is an important sense in which we respond to problems when we can personalize them—that is, when we view them as real events happening to real people. Figures about the number of homeless people are likely to be far less galvanizing than coming in contact with a hungry child sleeping in a public park.

It is always difficult to link public policy and individual need, but it is misleading to deny the linkage completely. For example, on a cold January night in 1987 two homeless people died on the streets of Los Angeles, and the city newspaper noted that their deaths were reported "one day after the City Council declined to act on a proposal to open city buildings to the homeless, and Mayor Tom Bradley appealed to the public to donate blankets to help keep them warm."[22] Should we be motivated by such cases? Perhaps it is more reasonable to adopt a somewhat calloused viewpoint, examining the statistics and making allocation decisions in a systematic and responsible way. After all, if I give money to this person on the street, perhaps it will be spent on drugs. If we give more welfare benefits to people in shelters, perhaps they will be less likely to look for apartments or for jobs.

We must all ask ourselves such questions, for there are consequences to our actions for which we are responsible. But we would hope that our responses, as individuals and as a society, will not be limited to such objectifying analyses of the long-term effects of each action. In spite of its moral ambiguity, there is something refreshing, healthy, and responsible about simply giving money to someone who asks us for it. To respond in a direct fashion to someone in need is to affirm (however briefly and tentatively) a unique contact with another person. It involves trusting the person to use the money wisely, or at least, simply defining the situation in a very raw and direct manner: I have some extra money, this person is asking me for it, and I can give it to him. Each of us has to decide how to respond, not only to the person in the street but to the broader homeless population who implicitly need assistance every day. Whatever our response, it is important that we think carefully, and feel deeply, before we turn away.

Such discussions force us to confront our own ambivalence in terms of the broader cultural tension between affectivity and neutrality discussed earlier in this chapter. Perhaps there is a moral choice to be made in such situations, since social values—ranging from self-protection to the busyness of our lives—certainly provide us with ample justification for turning aside. The fact that the tension is at the level of cultural values may mean that we have no easy solution; the choice is ours, and each of us makes it every day of our lives.

The obligation to respond is often phrased in more narrow legal terms, such as the assertion that there is a "right" to housing. Much attention is being given to this question, and the legal implications of the dispute are being fought out in courts throughout the nation. The way in which this question is resolved will have important consequences for the types of benefits the state will be expected to provide to homeless people. However important these questions are, we believe it is worth remembering that our obligations to people should not depend upon whether or not we consider them to have a legal right to the basic resources they need. Homeless people are still in need of shelter even if it is not defined as a basic constitutional right. As individuals, we must resist the tendency to turn every moral or social question into a purely legal or constitutional one. In the final analysis, the U.S. Supreme Court cannot help us with the decision each of us must make when we are approached by a homeless person on the street or when we step into a voting booth to decide whether our tax money should be spent on low-income housing.

One further aspect of the social dimension is particularly important in terms of our understanding of American society. One of our most cherished myths is our self-perception as a nation of being open to the stranger, the immigrant, the marginalized. This self-understanding is reflected in the words of Emma Lazarus inscribed on the Statue of Liberty: "Give me your tired, your poor, your huddled masses." It resides in the words of the key texts in the religious traditions that have helped form and foster the values of our society: "Let justice well up as waters, and righteousness as a mighty stream." It echoes in many of the social policies of the past fifty years, with their efforts (however insufficient) to provide help for the helpless, to use government as a means of final assistance to those who are outcasts and alienated.

However short we have always fallen of living up to this ideal, and however mixed it has always been with countervailing themes of bigotry and possessive individualism in American history, we believe few Americans are willing to give up on this set of cultural values completely. Indeed, the more aware we become of how far short we have fallen, the more likely we are to turn back to such values, to heed the prophetic voices in our past and our present who consistently called us back to their central role in our lives. Even in the midst of major economic problems and social malaise, the United States remains a country rich in both financial resources and a tradition of compassion and social responsibility.

If this remains part of our vision of American society, then the experiences of marginalized people such as homeless families serve to remind us of our own moral responsibilities. They undercut our all-too-easy assumptions about the social solidarity we would like our country to embody. It is not only (or, perhaps, even primarily) the dignity of the homeless themselves that is undermined by their continued status and treatment; it is our dignity as well. To feel a sense of obligation to respond to people who are homeless is, in large part, a recognition that our own dignity, our own status as human beings, is being touched and challenged by what happens to them. At its best, such an awareness is the highest calling to which we can attain, and the strongest reason to respond to the needs and rights of the least fortunate in our midst.

This book has been about dignity—about its importance, its undermining, and its reassertion. The homeless need to feel that they have dignity, just as the rest of us need to believe that the existence of homelessness does not undermine our moral standing as a people who care about each other. Although their struggle is the harsher one, ours may be equally important, for the answers we find will help define the nature and tone of our national moral sensibility. If we cannot commit ourselves to preventing homelessness, we can at least commit ourselves to recognizing that homeless people are like us in many ways and to acknowledging that our own autonomy can lead us to the sense of solidarity they so desperately seek with us.

Appendix 1

Characteristics of Sample

The interviews followed a structured list of questions (see appendix 3), with interviewees being invited to offer open-ended answers rather than respond to fixed-choice alternatives. The narrative portion of these interviews was transcribed, and from these transcriptions coding of selected responses was done. The following information summarizes this coding.

Sex of Respondents Who Were Interviewed
($n = 100$)

female = 87   male/female couples = 6
male = 7

Ethnicity of Respondents
($n = 100$)

Black = 49   Native American = 4
White = 28   Interracial = 2
Hispanic = 16   Filipino = 1

Marital Status of Respondents
($n = 100$)

single parent = 42   living with partner = 8
living with spouse = 28   separated = 8
spouse not in shelter = 14

Age of Respondents
(n = 99; 1 respondent did not provide age)

under 20 years = 6
20–29 years = 40
30–39 years = 38

40–49 years = 13
over 50 years = 2

Number of Children in Respondent Family Living in Shelter
(n = 100)

one child = 32
two children = 33
three children = 19
four children = 9

five children = 3
six children = 2
seven children = 1
thirteen children = 1

Education Level of Respondents
(n = 99; 1 respondent did not provide education level)

less than high school = 13
some high school = 20
high school graduate = 38

some college = 18
associate degree = 8
college degree = 2

Precipitating Causes of Homelessness of Respondents
(n = 100)

ran out of money = 37
relationship breakdown = 30
evicted (child-related) = 7
evicted (drug use) = 5

late welfare check = 5
medical problem = 3
unspecified = 13

Where Respondent Families Were Living Prior to Shelter
(n = 110; because some families spent time in more than one place)

another shelter = 33
car/park/street/beach = 22

hotel/motel = 55

History of Substance Abuse among Respondents

partner abused drugs = 31
partner alcoholic = 25

personally abused drugs = 25
personal alcohol problem = 6

History of Physical and Sexual Abuse among Respondents

physical abuse (as an adult) = 40
physical/sexual abuse (as a child) = 21

Appendix 2

Statistics on Homelessness in Los Angeles

The number of homeless in the United States, or in any specific urban area, is a matter of debate. The 1990 census, for example, stated that there were 228,621 homeless persons in the United States, of whom 49,081 were in California and 7,706 within the city limits of Los Angeles. Nationally, according to census figures, 178,828 persons resided in shelters and 49,793 were living on the streets (in places visible enough that census workers could count them). California led the nation with 31,000 people in shelters and 18,081 living on the streets. In Los Angeles there were 4,597 people residing in shelters and 3,109 on the streets.[1]

Homeless advocates, however, have criticized the census statistics as dramatically undercounting those without shelter. The census figures are approximately one-half the number offered by the Urban Institute, which estimates that there are 500,000 homeless. Other estimates range as high as a million or more. Part of the debate and confusion centers on whether one is counting the number of homeless on a given night versus the number that are homeless during the course of a year. Also, the census figures may underestimate the full scope of the housing problem because they focus on persons living in shelters and those visible to census counters but ignore individuals sleeping on the couches of friends or relatives or living in converted garages.[2]

In Los Angeles homeless advocates propose rather different figures. For example, the Shelter Partnership estimates that in 1990–91 there were between 125,600 and 204,000 people who were homeless during some portion of the year in Los Angeles County. On any given night, there are 38,420 to 68,670 people homeless, of whom approximately 15,000 are members of families (and approximately 11,000 are children). The number of homeless people in Los Angeles County increased by 15.9 percent over the previous year, and the 1989–90 figures for homelessness represented a 17.3 percent increase over 1988–89.[3]

Estimates of the number of homeless children are equally disputed. In one of the analyses (conducted in 1988), the U.S. General Accounting Office estimated that on any given night, "about 68,000 children and youths of age 16 and younger may be members of families that are literally homeless." Of this group, an estimated 25,500 were in urban shelters and hotels. In addition, this same study suggested that "nearly 186,000 children and youths may be precariously housed, spending the night in doubled-up ('shared housing') circumstances." (This study did not include homeless runaway children and youths.)[4]

In our opinion, disputes over the number of homeless people are not so significant as the fact that the number of homeless families is substantial and appears to be steadily increasing. Even using the lowest estimates, homelessness is a serious problem, and current public policy initiatives are clearly insufficient. These facts provide a sufficient incentive for concern and response, regardless of the specific numbers.

In response to the growing number of homeless during the last several years, shelters have seen a dramatic increase nationally. For example, a 1989 HUD study estimated that there were approximately 5,400 shelters in the United States, almost triple the number that had existed five years earlier. Thirty-six percent of these shelters served families with children, and 40 percent of the people living in shelters were members of homeless families. In Los Angeles in 1990, there were 7,938 shelter beds, representing a three-fold increase over 1984, when there were 2,452 shelter beds.[5] Los Angeles shelters operate at nearly 100 percent capacity, and according to a 1989 report the typical shelter in Los Angeles turned away more than 13 people a night, indicating that there may have been as many as 1,800 a night who were denied shelter.[6]

Provisions for homeless persons in Los Angeles are quite different from those in New York City, to take one point of comparison. In Los Angeles the system is operated principally by private nonprofit agencies that are sponsored by churches and other community groups. Although these shelters may draw on county, state, and federal funds for support, they also tend to exercise a great deal of autonomy in terms of how they operate. In 1990, according to the Shelter Partnership, 66 percent of shelter income came from public sources, while 34 percent was from private sources—but this represented a dramatic reversal from a few years ago when more than three-quarters of shelter income came from private sources.[7] This change obviously represents greater responsiveness by government agencies to the problem of homelessness, but it may also indicate that private donations simply cannot keep pace with the growing problem. When compared to New York City, L.A.'s shelter system is much more fragmented, with the burden for serving the homeless falling primarily on churches and other nonprofit agencies.[8]

The competition for low-income housing in Los Angeles is extremely keen. Hispanic immigrants have taken over many of the neighborhoods previously occupied by low-income blacks, a development partly responsible for a severe shortage of housing for blacks living at the poverty level. Los Angeles is a very dynamic community, and its minority populations are continually shifting. For example, areas that until recently were occupied by African Americans and then became primarily Hispanic are now being bought up by Koreans who have emigrated to Los Angeles. The bottom line is that housing is in desperately short supply, with vacancy rates being under 1 percent in many areas, and rental prices being very high. In many parts of the city it is virtually impossible to find a one- or two-bedroom apartment for under five hundred dollars a month.

Appendix 3

Interview Questions

The interviews were conducted in an open-ended conversational fashion in order to place the respondents at ease. As a result, the following questions represent key topics and issues covered in each interview, but they were not necessarily asked of all respondents in precisely the same words or at precisely the same point in the interview.

Family

1. How many children do you have?
2. What ages are they? Boys? Girls?
3. Are all of your children living with you? If not, where are they living? Are any in foster care, living with grandparents, or with a former spouse?
4. Are you married? [If so] Are you currently living with your husband [wife] or with someone else—or are you single now?
5. [If ethnicity is not obvious] What ethnic group do you identify with? (e.g., black, Hispanic, Asian, Native American, etc.)

Homelessness

1. What happened? When did you first become homeless? [probe for sequence of events]
2. So what went wrong? (e.g., job? family problems?)
3. Since you first became homeless, where have you been living? [probe for details: car, motels, street, shelter, with friends or relatives]
4. What have been some of your worst experiences since becoming homeless?
5. Who has been most helpful to you? [If parents are living] Have your parents been very supportive? How about relatives? Friends? Social service agencies? Churches or synagogues?

Assistance/Aid/Employment

1. What has been your main source of money since you have been homeless?
   A. Government programs: Food Stamps, AFDC, SSI, SDI, etc. Was it much of a hassle applying for any of these programs?

    B. Charitable programs: food pantries, churches, missions, etc.

    C. Gifts: from family, friends, strangers.

    D. Work: what type? for how long?

    E. I know that some people in your situation have to resort to prostitution or drug dealing in order to support their family. Have you had to?

2. What has been your main source of food during this time?

    A. Fast food outlets (e.g., McDonalds, Burger King)

    B. Markets (e.g., 7-Eleven, Vons)

    C. Food pantries, shelters, missions, etc.

Coping

1. How have you been doing during this time? Have you felt very depressed or anxious, or do you feel like you have been coping fairly well?

2. How have your kids been doing? Have they seemed upset, or are they doing okay?

3. [If school age] Have your kids been going to school?

4. How have you been doing as a family? Has your situation caused strains in your family? How have you and your kids been getting along? How have you and your husband/partner been getting along?

Background

1. Where were you born?

2. What year? [How old are you?]

3. Tell me what it was like growing up. [Did you live with relatives, foster parents, or in an institution?]

4. What kind of house(s) did you live in? Describe. Did your parents/relatives [or other persons you lived with] own or rent the place where you lived?

5. Was money a problem when you were growing up? How would you rate your family's income compared to others in your town or city (e.g., above average, average, below average)?

6. Was your family ever homeless?

7. Where did you go to school?

8. What is the highest grade that you completed? [If didn't finish high school: Did you get your GED?]

9. Have you had any special job training beyond what you received in school? (e.g., through union or government programs)

10. What would you say about your reading skills? Do you have problems filling out welfare forms and the like?

Employment

1. Please give me a sketch of jobs you have held. About how long were you employed at each? What was the approximate salary or hourly wage at each?

2. What about the jobs of men [women] you have lived with?

Abuse

1. As a child, did your parents or others beat you—more than the usual discipline most children receive? [By whom? At what age? Did it happen often?]
2. Were you ever sexually abused? [By whom? At what age? Did it happen often? Did you tell anyone?]

Housing

1. How old were you when you left home?
2. Where did you live after leaving home?
3. Have you ever owned a home?
4. What were you paying for rent immediately before you became homeless?
5. How difficult has it been for you to find low-cost housing?
6. In the past, what have you had to pay for housing for your family?
7. In your experience, have rent prices been increasing, staying about the same, or decreasing?

Health

1. Do you have any health problems now? What? For how long?
2. How about your children? Have they had any recent medical problems?
3. [If ill] What sort of treatment have you [your children] been getting? Has it been a problem to get, or to pay for, medical treatment?
4. Have you done a lot of drinking at different times in your life? How about recently? Has alcohol interfered with getting a job or taking care of your children?
5. Have you ever done drugs? Are you doing drugs now? [If so] How often? How do you pay for them? Have drugs interfered in your life very much?
6. People from all kinds of backgrounds have mental problems. Have you ever been in a mental hospital or wondered if you should get psychiatric help?

Citizenship/Arrest

1. [If an ethnic minority] Have you experienced any prejudice in getting a job? [If yes] Can you give me an example?
2. [If Hispanic] Has there been any problem getting a job because an employer questioned whether you were a citizen?
3. If a person has a prison record, it is sometimes tough getting a job. Has that been a problem for you or the men/women you have lived with?

Religion

1. How good a job do you think religious groups are doing in helping people who are having housing problems?
2. Have you received any help from church or religiously sponsored food pantries or shelters? How about for your children?
3. Do you think God is very concerned about your situation, or do you feel pretty much abandoned by God?

Future

1. What are your immediate plans? Especially in terms of housing after you leave this shelter? And how about employment?
2. Do you have any recommendations for those involved in social services or religiously supported shelters? What would be of most help to people in your situation?
3. When you think about the future, what do you imagine things will be like for you in five years, ten years?
4. What have we not talked about that you think is important?

Notes

Preface

1. Kay Young McChesney, "Women Without: Homeless Mothers and Their Children" (Ph.D. diss., University of Southern California, 1987).

Chapter 1: Families

1. Lisa Klee Mihaly, *Homeless Families: Failed Policies and Young Victims* (Washington, D.C.: Children's Defense Fund, 1991), p. 2.

2. See Rick Beard, ed., *On Being Homeless: Historical Perspectives* (New York: Museum of the City of New York, 1987).

3. *The Stanford Studies of Homeless Families, Children, and Youth* (Stanford Center for the Study of Families, Children, and Youth, 1991), pp. 11–13. This study will hereafter be cited as *Stanford Study*. Because of the size of the sample, and the fact that it is a California study covering approximately the same period as our research (1990–91), this study will serve as a valuable comparison throughout this chapter to our findings and observations.

4. Kathleen Hirsch, *Songs from the Alley* (New York: Ticknor and Fields, 1989), p. xi.

5. Mihaly states: "Homelessness is not a permanent condition. Most families are homeless for less than thirty days. Fully 70 percent of the families interviewed by HUD in 1988 had been homeless for less than three months. Similarly, 82 percent of the families in Minnesota's shelters in 1990 had been homeless for less than one month, as had half of the homeless families in West Virginia in 1989. The duration of a family's homelessness is affected by numerous factors, most importantly the availability of services to help it return to permanent housing, the job market, and the supply of low-cost housing in its community" (*Homeless Families*, p. 3).

6. *Stanford Study*, p. 12.

7. *Stanford Study*, pp. 10–11.

8. In comparing homeless families with poor (but housed) at-risk families, the Stanford study found substantial differences between these two groups in terms of their respective levels of social support. The at-risk families had much stronger social support networks, indicating that they could stay about three times longer with their parents, siblings, and other relatives than could homeless families (p. 15).

9. *Housing Los Angeles: Affordable Housing for the Future* (Los Angeles: Blue Ribbon Committee for Affordable Housing, December 1988), p. 5.

10. Ibid., p. 11.

11. Mihaly, *Homeless Families,* pp. 10–11.

12. Ibid., p. 5.

13. The federal government stated that in 1990 a family of four needed to earn $13,359 in order to be above the poverty line. However, someone earning $5 an hour who works a forty-hour week, twelve months a year, only grosses $10,400.

14. Mihaly, *Homeless Families,* pp. 11.

15. Frank Clifford, "Rich-Poor Gulf Widens in State," *Los Angeles Times,* May 11, 1992, p. A-1.

16. Mihaly, *Homeless Families,* p. 12.

17. Ibid.

18. See, for example, Bassuk and Rosenberg, "Why Does Family Homelessness Occur? A Case-Control Study," *American Journal of Public Health* 78, no. 7 (1988): 783–88.

19. All participants in this study were promised complete confidentiality, and although the interviews were tape-recorded, code numbers (rather than names) were placed on the cassette tapes. We originally had participants sign release forms for the interviews, but some participants objected to this because the form contained their name and therefore constituted a record of who was interviewed. Subsequently we appealed to the Human Subjects Review Board at the University of Southern California, which had required signed releases, and it agreed to verbal consent by the study participants.

20. Eighty-seven of the interviews were conducted with single women, seven with single men, and the remaining six with couples.

21. The one difficulty we encountered was that individuals did not always keep the interview appointments. Frequently it was the case that although four or five interviews might be scheduled by shelter staff, only two or three persons would show up. In our judgment, this was not out of hostility toward the study but rather a result of the fact that many of the participants did not live by appointment books and schedules, and they simply forgot to come or had to attend to job searching or child care. Initially we had planned two hundred interviews and six-month follow-up interviews after the participants had left the shelter. Budget restraints required that we limit the study to one hundred interviews with no follow-up.

22. Because of the selection process in these shelters, and because intact homeless families tend to be emotionally more stable, our sample does not include severely mentally ill persons, who do comprise a substantial proportion of the homeless population as a whole. In addition, we would expect that the people we interviewed were probably among the more stable and responsible residents of the shelters we visited, since they were the ones more likely to keep appointments and be willing to speak about their problems. At the same time, it is also possible that many of the more enterprising and assertive residents were too busy seeking work or alternative housing during the day to be able or willing to take the time to speak with us.

23. In their study of two northern California counties (Santa Clara and San Mateo),

the Stanford investigators found the following: "Thirty-six percent of the homeless families were Hispanics of Mexican descent, 29% were non-Hispanic Whites, and 25% were African Americans" (*Stanford Study,* pp. 10–11).

24. In terms of ethnic breakdown, our sample is very close to that reported in a 1990 study by the U.S. Conference of Mayors, which found the following: 46 percent of the homeless population is black, 34 percent is Anglo, 15 percent is Hispanic, and 4 percent is other minorities. Laura DeKoven Waxman and Lilia M. Reyes, *A Status Report on Homeless Families in America's Cities,* 1990.

25. In the Stanford study, 52 percent of the families interviewed were headed by single parents, while 30 percent involved children living with both biological parents (pp. 12–13).

26. The Stanford study found that the average homeless family had 2.3 children, with Hispanic families having 2.8 children compared to 1.9 for non-Hispanic whites. They report that 29 percent of the homeless mothers were under eighteen years old when their first child was born, leading them to conclude that for most families homelessness was not the result of early parenthood (p. 13).

27. This number may be even higher since several people said that they did not know whether their home was rented or owned by their parents.

28. The Stanford researchers found that 34 percent of the homeless parents they interviewed reported a history of substance abuse. Whites (63 percent) had the highest rate of substance abuse, compared with 36 percent for African Americans and 18 percent for Hispanics. Substance abuse, however, was found to be no lower among poor at-risk families than homeless families, leading the researchers to seek other causes for homelessness.

Chapter 3: The Welfare System

1. "What Kind of Sense Is This?" (editorial), *Los Angeles Times,* Oct. 3, 1989, p. II-6.

2. Lanie Jones, "Youngsters Share Plight of Homeless," *Los Angeles Times,* May 19, 1987, pp. I-1, I-25.

3. National Coalition for the Homeless, *Over the Edge* (July 1988), p. 2.

4. Such a model is in keeping with the well-known rules of charity associated with Maimonides, in which the anonymity of both giver and receiver occupies a very high place in the order of charity. Indeed, the only stage higher than this is to provide the resources for poor persons to support themselves.

Chapter 4: Shelters

1. This image is drawn from a conversation with Melinda Bird, a poverty law advocate in Los Angeles.

2. This figure is based on an estimate from a staff member at Infoline, one of the major referral services in Los Angeles County.

3. For a more detailed analysis, refer to the very interesting discussion of this issue in F. Stevens Redburn and Terry F. Buss, *Responding to America's Homeless* (New York: Praeger, 1986).

4. Rene Jahiel, "The Situation of Homelessness," in *The Homeless in Contemporary Society*, ed. Richard Bingham, Roy Green, and Sammis White (Newbury Park, Calif.: Sage, 1987), p. 107.

5. Jones, "Youngsters Share Plight of Homeless."

6. As indicated earlier, fifty-five of the respondents had stayed in a hotel or motel before moving to the shelter, and twenty-two had spent at least one night on a park bench, beach, or street or in a parked car.

7. Miles Corwin, "Man's Idea to Aid Homeless Lands Him in the Doghouse," *Los Angeles Times*, Apr. 23, 1989, pp. I-3, I-16.

8. Frank Clifford and Penelope McMillan, "Homeless Tally Overstated for L.A., Study Shows," *Los Angeles Times*, Feb. 8, 1987, pp. I-1, I-29, I-30; Clifford and McMillan, "Bradley Says He's Responsible for Skid Row Raids," *Los Angeles Times*, Feb. 20, 1987, pp. II-1, II-3; Dean Murphy, "Tentative Pact Reached in Skid Row Sweeps," *Los Angeles Times*, Mar. 15, 1987, p. II-1; Frederick Muir, "Police Try to Confine Skid Row Homeless to Areas by Missions," *Los Angeles Times*, Feb. 10, 1989, pp. II-1, II-8; Muir, "City to Roll Back Disputed Police Skid Row Sweeps," *Los Angeles Times*, Feb. 17, 1989, pp. II-1, II-3.

9. HUD survey, pp. 21–23.

10. Institute of Medicine, *Homelessness, Health, and Human Needs* (Washington, D.C.: National Academy Press, 1988), pp. 32–33.

11. Committee on Shelter Standards, *Los Angeles Shelter Standards* (draft), January 1988, p. 5.

12. The HUD survey provides an excellent overview of the services provided nationwide by the shelter system.

Chapter 5: Coping with Being Homeless

1. The analogy to addictions such as alcoholism should be obvious. For example, overcoming denial is the first of the twelve steps associated with Alcoholics Anonymous' approach.

Chapter 6: Finding Meaning in Being Homeless

1. Discussions of American civil religion have focused on the ways in which both explicit and implicit religious symbols play major roles in our everyday lives. For a particularly interesting example, see the essays in Russell E. Richey and Donald G. Jones, eds., *American Civil Religion* (New York: Harper and Row, 1974).

2. Max Weber was one of the first social theorists to recognize the importance of theodicy questions in motivating individuals and societies, as well as the ways in which these questions are dependent upon a particular conception of God.

Chapter 7: The Concept of Dignity

1. Peter Berger, "On the Obsolescence of the Concept of Honor," in *The Homeless Mind: Modernization and Consciousness*, ed. Peter Berger, Brigitte Berger, and Hansfried Kellner (New York: Random House, 1973), p. 89 (essay first published in 1970). It is worth noting that Berger is highly critical of the fact that modern society focuses on the concept of dignity to the exclusion of terms such as honor.

2. The amount of literature in the human rights arena is enormous. Key documents pertaining to U.S. and international law can be found in House of Representatives, Committee on Foreign Affairs, *Human Rights Documents* (Washington, D.C.: Government Printing Office, 1983). For a particularly useful overview of some basic human rights issues as they are worked out in international law, see Oscar Schachter's discussion in "Editorial Comment: Human Dignity as a Normative Concept," in *American Journal of International Law* 77 (October 1983): 848-54.

3. One of the continuing debates about the interpretation of John Calvin's understanding of human nature, for example, concerns the extent to which he maintains some continuing ability of human beings to recognize good and evil without being overwhelmed by the Fall. This interpretation is particularly important given the influence of the Calvinistic tradition on the formation of American religious and social values in the colonial period. For a fascinating account of Calvin's vestigial theory of natural law, see David Little, "Calvin and the Prospects for a Christian Theory of Natural Law," in *Norm and Context in Christian Ethics,* ed. Gene Outka and Paul Ramsey (New York: Charles Scribner's Sons, 1968), pp. 175-97.

4. The Roman Catholic tradition has been particularly concerned with an explicitly theological and social understanding of dignity. This concern is expressed most strongly in a series of papal encyclicals that emerged during the past one hundred years. For two brief reviews, both of which provide fine discussions of the human rights tradition in various contexts, see Yale Task Force on Population Ethics, "Moral Claims, Human Rights, and Population Policies," *Theological Studies* 35 (March 1974): 83-113; and Alfred Hennelly, S.J., and John Langan, S.J., eds., *Human Rights in the Americas* (Washington, D.C.: Georgetown University Press, 1982).

5. Michael Walzer, *Spheres of Justice: A Defense of Pluralism and Equality* (New York: Basic Books, 1983), pp. 277-78.

6. From certain religious perspectives, the conferral is made by God, and the "social" dimension may involve merely the relationship between human and divine. But the basic point remains the same: I do not merely create my own dignity, nor do I maintain my sense of dignity without some connection with other(s) who both bestow and acknowledge that dignity.

7. We are indebted to Russell Ayres for this reminder.

Chapter 8: Dignity and the Homeless Person

1. Bruce Vladeks and Ellen Bassuk, "The Shame of Homelessness in America," *Los Angeles Times,* Oct. 16, 1988, pp. V-2, V-6.

2. Jonathan Kozol, *Rachel and Her Children: Homeless Families in America* (New York: Fawcett Columbine, 1988), p. 130.

3. Institute of Medicine, *Homelessness, Health, and Human Needs,* p. 32.

4. Ellen L. Bassuk, "Homeless Families: Single Mothers and Their Children in Boston Shelters," in *The Mental Health Needs of Homeless Persons,* ed. Ellen L. Bassuk (San Francisco: Jossey-Bass, 1986), p. 52.

5. Our criticism of welfare workers can be no more harsh than our criticism, for example, of surgeons who build emotional barriers between themselves and their suffering patients.

6. Peter Marin, "Go Ask Alice," *Los Angeles Times*, Feb. 1, 1987, pp. I-6, I-8.

7. For more detailed discussions, see David Schwartz and John Glascock, *Combating Homelessness: A Resource Book* (New Brunswick, N.J.: Rutgers University, American Affordable Housing Institute, n.d.), p. 85.

8. This sort of analysis of cultural values stands in the tradition of social theorists such as Robert Merton and Talcott Parsons, among others; many of the values identified in our discussion derive from their writings. More recently, Robert Bellah and his associates emphasize many of these ambivalent values in *Habits of the Heart: Individualism and Commitment in American Life* (New York: Harper and Row, 1985). On a more individual level, the writings of Erik Erikson direct our attention to the tensions that confront us at various stages of our development.

9. Among the more compelling critiques of American individualism are Philip Slater, *The Pursuit of Loneliness* (Boston: Beacon Press, 1970); Christopher Lasch, *The Culture of Narcissism* (New York: W. W. Norton, 1978); and Bellah et al., *Habits of the Heart*.

10. Historically, for example, the strongly communitarian instincts and theologies of the Puritan strand of American colonialism must be placed in contrast to the images of the individualistic pioneer.

11. Bellah et al., *Habits of the Heart*, pp. 150–51.

12. It should be clear by now, to readers familiar with some of the debates concerning the philosophy of justice and modern liberalism, that the authors are sympathetic to the approach of John Rawls. It should be noted, however, that we would ground the fundamental commitment to dignity (or to "self-respect," in Rawls's sense) in a religious commitment rather than a purely philosophical one. (See Rawls, *A Theory of Justice* [Harvard University Press, 1971].)

13. At a religious level, the rediscovery of a more "passive" orientation is being rediscovered by Christian writers who emphasize the paradox of God's power as revealed in the powerlessness of the death of Jesus Christ. For a particularly powerful and moving treatment of this theme, see W. H. Vanstone, *The Stature of Waiting*.

14. *Talcott Parsons, The Social System* (New York: Free Press, 1951), especially chapter 3. In spite of the dated nature of the writing and the narrowly functionalist approach, Parsons's discussion remains a brilliant evocation of many of the underlying themes that continue to define American social values.

15. Philip Slater makes a related point concerning the somewhat more troubling aspects of restlessness and extreme individualism in the American character in *The Pursuit of Loneliness*.

16. Schachter, "Editorial Comment," p. 852 (emphasis added).

17. Perhaps this is the significance of the often ill-used statement (attributed to Jesus) that we will always have the poor with us. To believe that we could live in a world where we are not confronted with people in need is to step outside of any world in which any of us are likely to live.

18. Jill Stewart, "Proposition 3 Loss Spurs Search to Save Housing," *Los Angeles Times*, Apr. 19, 1989, pp. II-1, II-8.

19. Edmund Newton, " 'New Realism' Hardens Attitudes Toward Homeless," *Los Angeles Times*, Oct. 16, 1989, pp. B-1, B-6.

20. Ibid.

21. Charles Hoch, "A Brief History of the Homeless Problem in the United States," in *The Homeless in Contemporary Society,* ed. Richard Bingham, Roy Green, and Sammis White (Newbury Park, Calif.: Sage, 1987), p. 28.

22. Carol McGraw and Jill Stewart, "Deaths of Two Homeless Linked to Nighttime Cold," *Los Angeles Times,* Jan. 18, 1987, pp. I-1, I-2.

Appendix 2: Statistics on Homelessness in Los Angeles

1. Sam Fulwood III, "Census Workers Count 228,621 Homeless across U.S.," *Los Angeles Times,* Apr. 13, 1991, p. A-19.

2. Perhaps the most thorough and balanced treatment of the scale of the homeless problem is found in Peter H. Rossi's masterful book *Down and Out in America* (Chicago: University of Chicago Press, 1989). Rossi suggests that the best overall estimate of the number of people homeless each night is between 300,000 and 500,000 (p. 70).

3. Shelter Partnership, *The Number of Homeless People in Los Angeles City and County, July 1990 to June 1991* (Los Angeles, May 1992), p. 1. Shelter Partnership, Inc., is located at 1010 S. Flower Street, Suite 400, Los Angeles, CA 90015.

4. U.S. General Accounting Office, *Children and Youths: About 68,000 Homeless and 186,000 in Shared Housing at Any Given Time,* GAO–PEMD-89-14 (Washington, D.C., June 1989).

5. Shelter Partnership, *Short-Term Housing Directory of Los Angeles* (Los Angeles, Fall 1990).

6. Shelter Partnership, *Homelessness and the Short-Term Housing System of Los Angeles* (Los Angeles, October 1989). We cannot determine, however, whether there were multiple denials for the same person requesting access to numerous shelters on the same night.

7. Ibid., p. 4.

8. This characteristic of how Los Angeles deals with its homeless has obvious liabilities, but it has also led to a somewhat entrepreneurial effort in serving the homeless population. Currently there is a very active program in Los Angeles to renovate housing on Skid Row. Churches, temples, and various philanthropic groups are buying hotels and refurbishing them, utilizing public as well as corporate funding. Executives from prominent legal firms and other businesses in the city are involved in many of these partnerships with private nonprofit groups. Rooms are rented to low-income people at affordable prices, and hotels also offer some social services to residents. The intended audience for these hotels is single men and women, rather than families. Families find it much more difficult to get housing.

Selected Bibliography

Barak, Gregg. *Gimme Shelter: A Social History of Homelessness in Contemporary America.* New York: Praeger, 1991.

Bassuk, Ellen L., "Homeless Families: Single Mothers and Their Children in Boston Shelters." In *The Mental Health Needs of Homeless Persons,* ed. Ellen L. Bassuk, 45–54. San Francisco: Jossey-Bass, 1986.

———. "The Feminization of Homelessness: Homeless Families in Boston Shelters." *American Journal of Social Psychiatry* 7, no. 1 (1987): 19–23.

———. "Redefining Transitional Housing for Homeless Families." *Yale Law and Policy Review* 6, no. 2 (1988): 309–30.

Bassuk, Ellen L., and E. M. Gallagher. "The Impact of Homelessness on Children." *Child and Youth Services* 14, no. 1 (1990): 19–33.

Bassuk, Ellen L., and L. Rosenberg. "Why Does Family Homelessness Occur? A Case-Control Study." *American Journal of Public Health* 78, no. 7 (1988): 783–88.

Bassuk, E. L., and L. Rubin. "Homeless Children: A Neglected Population." *American Journal of Orthopsychiatry* 57, no. 2 (1987): 279–86.

Bassuk, Ellen L., L. Rubin, and A. S. Lauriat. "Characteristics of Sheltered Homeless Families." *American Journal of Public Health* 76, no. 9 (September 1986): 1097–1101.

Battle, S. F. "Homeless Women and Children: The Question of Poverty." *Child and Youth Services* 14, no. 1 (1990): 111–27.

Belcher, John R. *Helping the Homeless: Where Do We Go from Here?* Lexington, Mass.: Lexington Books, 1990.

Bellah, Robert, Richard Madsen, William Sullivan, Ann Swidler, and Steven Tipton. *Habits of the Heart: Individualism and Commitment in American Life.* New York: Harper and Row, 1985.

Berger, Peter. "On the Obsolescence of the Concept of Honor." In *The Homeless Mind: Modernization and Consciousness,* ed. Peter Berger, Brigitte Berger, and Hansfried Kellner, 83–96. New York: Random House, 1973.

Blau, Joel. *The Invisible Poor: Homelessness in the United States* (New York: Oxford University Press, 1992).

Blue Ribbon Committee for Affordable Housing, City of Los Angeles. *Housing Los Angeles: Affordable Housing for the Future.* December 1988.

Boxill, Nancy A., and A. L. Beaty. "Mother/Child Interaction among Homeless Women and Their Children in a Public Night Shelter in Atlanta, Georgia." *Child and Youth Services* 14, no. 1 (1986): 49–64.

Burt, Martha. *Over the Edge: The Growth of Homelessness in the 1980s.* New York: Russell Sage Foundation, 1992.

Burt, M. R., and B. E. Cohen. "Differences among Homeless Single Women, Women with Children, and Single Men." *Social Problems* 36, no. 5 (1989): 508–24.

Caton, Carol L. M., ed. *Homelessness in America.* Oxford: Oxford University Press, 1990.

Coates, Robert. *A Street Is Not a Home.* Buffalo, N.Y.: Prometheus Books, 1990.

Committee on Shelter Standards. *Los Angeles Shelter Standards* (draft). Los Angeles, January 1988.

Dear, Michael J. and Jennifer Wolch. *Landscapes of Despair: From Deinstitutionalization to Homelessness.* Princeton, N.J.: Princeton University Press, 1987.

Erickson, Jon, and Charles Wilhelm, eds. *Housing the Homeless in Contemporary Society.* Newbury Park, Calif.: Sage, 1987.

Erikson, Erik. *Identity, Youth, and Crisis.* New York: W. W. Norton, 1968.

Fox, E. R., and L. Roth. "Homeless Children: Philadelphia as a Case Study." *Annals of the American Academy of Political and Social Science* 506 (1989): 141–51.

Giamo, Benedict, and Jeffrey Grunberg. *Beyond Homelessness: Frames of Reference.* Iowa City: University of Iowa Press, 1992.

Golden, Stephanie. *The Women Outside: Means and Myths of Homelessness.* Berkeley: University of California Press, 1992.

Hall, J. A., and P. L. Maza. "No Fixed Address: The Effects of Homelessness on Families and Children." *Child and Youth Services* 14, no. 1 (1990): 35–47.

Hennelly, Alfred, and John Langan, eds. *Human Rights in the Americas.* Washington, D.C.: Georgetown University Press, 1982.

Hirsch, Kathleen. *Songs from the Alley.* New York: Ticknor and Fields, 1989.

Hoch, Charles. "A Brief History of the Homeless Problem in the United States." In *The Homeless in Contemporary Society,* ed. Richard Bingham, Roy Green, and Sammis White, 16–32. Newbury Park, Calif.: Sage, 1987.

Institute of Medicine. *Homelessness, Health, and Human Needs.* Washington, D.C.: National Academy Press, 1988.

Jahiel, Rene. "The Situation of Homelessness." In *The Homeless in Contemporary Society,* ed. Richard Bingham, Roy Green, and Sammis White, 99–118. Newbury Park, Calif.: Sage, 1987.

Kozol, Jonathan. *Rachel and Her Children: Homeless Families in America.* New York: Fawcett Columbine, 1988.

Lang, Michael H. *Homelessness amid Affluence: Structure and Paradox in the American Political Economy.* New York: Praeger, 1989.

Lasch, Christopher. *The Culture of Narcissism.* New York: W. W. Norton, 1978.

Little, David. "Calvin and the Prospects for a Christian Theory of Natural Law." In *Norm and Context in Christian Ethics,* ed. Gene Outka and Paul Ramsey, 175–97. New York: Charles Scribner's Sons, 1968.

Mascari, D. "Homeless Families: Do They Have a Right to Integrity?" *UCLA Law Review* 35, no. 159 (1987): 159–206.

Merton, Robert K. *Sociological Ambivalence and Other Essays.* New York: Free Press, 1976.

Mihaly, Lisa Klee. *Homeless Families: Failed Policies and Young Victims.* Washington, D.C.: Children's Defense Fund, 1991.

Minnema, Theodore. "Human Dignity and Human Dependence." *Calvin Theological Journal* 16 (April 1981): 5–14.

National Coalition for the Homeless, *Over the Edge* (July 1988).

Parsons, Talcott. *The Social System.* New York: Free Press, 1951.

Redburn, F. Stevens and Terry F. Buss. *Responding to America's Homeless: Public Policy Alternatives.* New York: Praeger, 1986.

Rossi, Peter H. *Down and Out in America: The Origins of Homelessness.* Chicago: University of Chicago Press, 1989.

Schachter, Oscar. "Editorial Comment: Human Dignity as a Normative Concept." *American Journal of International Law* 77 (October 1983): 848–54.

Schwartz, David, and John Glascock. *Combating Homelessness: A Resource Book.* New Brunswick, N.J.: Rutgers University, American Affordable Housing Institute, n.d.

Shelter Partnership. *Homelessness and the Short-Term Housing System of Los Angeles.* Los Angeles, October 1989.

———. *The Number of Homeless People in Los Angeles City and County.* July 1990 to June 1991. Los Angeles, May 1992.

———. *Short-Term Housing Directory of Los Angeles.* Los Angeles, Fall 1990.

Slater, Philip. *The Pursuit of Loneliness.* Boston: Beacon Press, 1970.

The Stanford Studies of Homeless Families, Children, and Youth. Stanford Center for the Study of Families, Children, and Youth, 1991.

Stone, Michael. *One-Third of a Nation: A New Look at Housing Affordability in America.* Economic Policy Institute, 1990.

Stoner, Madeleine R. *Inventing a Non-Homeless Future: A Public Policy Agenda for Preventing Homelessness.* New York: P. Lang, 1989.

Thomas, Kenneth P. *The Number of Homeless People in Los Angeles County, July 1989 to June 1990.* December 19, 1990. Los Angeles: Shelter Partnership.

United States Conference of Mayors. *A Status Report on Homeless Families in America's Cities.* 1990.

United States General Accounting Office. *Children and Youths: About 68,000 Homeless and 186,000 in Shared Housing at Any Given Time.* GAO–PEMD-89-14. Washington, D.C., June 1989.

United States House of Representatives, Committee on Foreign Affairs. *Human Rights Documents.* Washington, D.C.: Government Printing Office, September 1983.

Vanstone, W. H. *The Stature of Waiting.* New York: Harper Collins, 1983.

Walzer, Michael. *Spheres of Justice: A Defense of Pluralism and Equality.* New York: Basic Books, 1983.

Wright, James D. *Address Unknown: The Homeless in America.* New York: A. de Gruyter, 1989.

Yale Task Force on Population Ethics. "Moral Claims, Human Rights, and Population Policies." *Theological Studies* 35 (March 1974): 83–113.

Index

BARRY JAY SELTSER, a senior social science analyst at the U.S. General Accounting Office, previously was on the faculties of the University of Southern California and Indiana University. He is the author of *Principles and Practice of Political Compromise: A Case Study of the United States Senate*.

DONALD E. MILLER is an associate professor of religion at the University of Southern California and the coauthor with Barry Jay Seltser of *Writing and Research in Religious Studies*. He is also coauthor with Lorna Touryan Miller of *Survivors: An Oral History of the Armenian Genocide*.